Japanese Pop Culture

Discovering the fascinating Japanese pop culture

The Land of Manga and Anime

DINGO

BOOK CLUB

www.DingoPublishing.com

Table of Contents

Introduction

Japan is an island nation replete with densely populated cities, the power of ancient Imperialism still looming large, thousands of temples and shrines, mountains, volcanoes, samurais and more. For some time, Japan was a powerful empire backed by her military and industrial strength.

Like all things in the world, the empire withered over time and, for various reasons. But that did not stop the country from retaining its powers. The country simply shifted its gaze on the world horizon from military and industrialization to something far more potent than economics and arms; popular culture. Its territorial powers are now evident in almost living room through the television, and in everyone's ears through their headphones.

Look at the way icons from popular Japanese culture have invaded the western world. Right from movies to manga to highly entertaining and popular cartoon characters to music to anime; Japanese pop culture has contributed significantly to the world pop culture, especially the western world.

Even Walt Disney borrowed one of his earliest comic characters from Japan; so believe nerds and experts of the cartoon and manga world. Remember the popular Hollywood sci-fi movie, *Big Hero 6*, based on a superhero team of Marvel Comics of the same name? The comic characters, the setting, and the movie borrowed heavily from Japanese manga books.

But this phenomenon of western culture borrowing from old Japanese cultures is not new. It has been taking place for some time now. A legendary story connects John Ford, the famed American director, and Akira Kurosawa, the equally famed Japanese film director. John Ford is believed to have visited the sets of a film directed by the not-yet-famous Kurosawa after WWII.

As he was leaving the set, the American is said to have told one of the staffs on the set to 'pass his regards to the director. However, 13 years later, when Kurosawa walked into one of John Ford's films sets, the entire crew and cast gave a standing ovation to the Japanese filmmaker. The horrible war, and it's even more terrible effects, did little to break the bond between two great artists.

That was then, and this is now! The post-war citizens of the western world have basked under the effects of the glorious Rising Sun. Nearly every childhood and teenage craze can be traced to Japan; whether Power Rangers, Pokémon, Transformers, Tamagotchi, and more.

All these characters from Japanese pop culture have broken every geographical barrier, at least in the world of media. One of the primary reasons for this outburst of Japanese pop culture all across the western world is MONEY. Yes, money did, does, and will continue to play an important role in the cross-mingling of cultures. A few purists treat art emerging from boardrooms with a bit of disdain. However, there is no need to be cynical about this phenomenon. While money might help in giving the right boost initially, the quality of products is a key element in sustaining interest and engagement among the masses. Japan's cultural sector is easily one that focuses on quality and innovation to keep alive world engagement.

A classic example is the case of the Japanese company, Nintendo, the producer and promoter of Pokémon video games, and the bouncing plumber, Mario. The popularity of the characters and consoles designed from the boardrooms of Nintendo has continued to draw crowds from every nook and corner of the world. Living in intricately detailed worlds, the video games and characters of Japanese pop culture needed more than money to achieve lasting global popularity.

Japanese pop culture is not just surviving, but also thriving, and that too in today's highly competitive world in which popularity is easily and casually torn asunder if requisite standards of quality and innovation are not met. To do this, pop culture from Japan needed more than just money and boardroom discussions. It needed a set of committed people willing to break creativity barriers every time to meet the exacting standards of the modern world.

And yet, despite the modernization of pop culture characters, they have managed to retain the fantasy and folklore foundations of Japan. Every child's dream pencil-box and lunch-box has a character from manga folklore; perhaps, a bit westernized, but still Japanese in origin.

And it is not just western kids who are fascinated by the popular culture offered by Japan. Even adults love what comes from the island nation. Otherwise, how did the gripping mystery stories of Masahiko Matsumoto become popular in the west way back in the 1950s? Today, this little known cartoonist's work has been translated into English and the Western adults love all of them.

Many of the anime series of Japanese pop culture are aimed as much at adults as at children. Gory, violent, and yet gripping, only Japan's creative minds can convert comics or manga written in their language into something that adults would get addicted to.

This book traces the history of Japanese pop culture through the following elements (in the same order), and their impact on the Western World:

1. Movies

2. TV shows

3. Anime

4. Manga

Let's get right on with it.

Chapter 1:
Japanese Movies & Impact on the Western World

On September 2, 1945, Japan officially accepted defeat in World War II and surrendered to the US. This Japanese surrender heralded an effective completion of the war. Japan may have lost its military dominance in the world, but they were to become a dominant player in a more powerful and widespread aspect of humankind- popular culture.

Japan started its conquer of pop culture global with its outstanding movies made by even better directors. Despite the US occupying and taking control of the country and its culture immediately after September 2, 1945, subduing the long history and heritage of Japan from creeping in and taking over world pop culture was impossible.

Let us look at the history of Japanese cinema and see how it impacted the western world. Cinema in Japan can easily be categorized as those films made before WWII, those made during WWII, and those made after WWII.

Japanese Cinema before WWII

The history of films in Japan can be dated back to the 18th century when the Dutch first introduced the concept of 'magic lantern.' The Japanese people manifested their creativity and the magic lantern became a very popular form of village art in the 19th century.

They used rear lighting and shadow puppets to show demons, ghosts and skeletons. The early magic lantern 'horror films' (called phantasmagoria theater) were all centered on these ghostly concepts taken from the myths and legends of ancient Japan.

Then, in 1897, a cameraman employed with Lumiere Brothers (the French inventors of the first motion picture camera), made a film on the sights of Tokyo which was the first film made in Japan. In the early 20th century, the film theaters in Japan had screen pictures (silent films) with narrators, called the benshi, who introduced the film and spoke in the characters' voices in the background.

The benshis were so popular in Japan that the era of Japanese silent films outlasted the American counterpart by an entire decade. American silent films were slowly but surely replaced by 'talkies' by the 1920s whereas the Japanese films continued to flourish until the 1930s, thanks to the versatility and creativity of the benshis.

Samurai films of these times were the most popular ones. These period silent films referred to as jidaigeki had anti-hero protagonists. They were based mostly in the Edo period (1603 A.D. – 1868 A.D.) though some were set in the later Heian or Meiji periods. Famous directors of these times include Masahiro Makino and Daisuke Ito. They created fast-paced samurai movies which were compared to rhythmic dancing. The films garnered both commercial success as well as critical acclaim.

The government took a lot of interest in film-making and, by the 1930s, and it compelled filmmakers to create promotional and propaganda documentaries called bunka eiga, a phrase translated from *Kulturfilm*, a similar film genre in Germany. The Kulturfilm genre was very popular and influential in Germany, contributing significantly to the rise and growth of the Nazi Party.

Japanese Movies during World War II

WWII and Japanese cinema are closely interlinked, and therefore, we should spend some time on the effects and aftermath of the war. Although the official start of World War II is considered as the point when Germany invaded Poland in 1939, Japan was already at war against its ancient rival, China, since July 1937. Beijing fell to Japan, and by December 1937, they captured Nanking, the capital of China at the same time.

During this time, the Japanese government controlled all domestic aspects in the country including health, education, advertising, news, public events, and, of course, cinema. It increased its demand for bunka eiga films, and any director or filmmaker who ridiculed or opposed military action or showcased the cruelty of war through exaggerated depiction' was suppressed. The films that the government found offensive or antinational were banned.

Japanese fairy tale 'Momotaro', lithograph,
published in 1889

Momotaro's Sea Eagles and Divine Sea Warriors –
Classic examples of bunka eiga films are Momotaro's *Sea Eagles*, a 37-minute film, made in 1943, and its sequel *Divine Sea Warriors*, an animated black-and-white film made in 1945.

Momotaro's Sea Eagles - The character of Momotaro, the peach boy, is based on a famous folklore of the same name in which a boy miraculously born from a peach grows up to become a great warrior. In this bunka eiga genre film, Momotaro is a brave commander of the Imperial Japanese Navy who is sent on a mission to attack and conquer Demon Island.

The setting of the Demon Island is clearly based on Pearl Harbor and Oahu leaving no doubt about which Japanese attack is being represented in the film. Momotaro sends a cute monkey and a cuddly puppy as soldiers to attack the Demon Island. This film and its sequel, *Divine Sea Warriors,* are believed to be among those very few surviving Japanese anime films of the 1940s. Many others were lost during the war and later on.

Momotaro's Divine Sea Warriors - The 1945 74-minute long *Divine Sea Warriors* was also written and directed by

Mitsuyo Seo. This propaganda film featured four cuddly animals including a bear cub, monkey, pheasant, and rabbit.

After their naval training, these four cuddly friends returned home to say goodbye to their families before going off to war. The action of the film is on an island in the Pacific Ocean where Momotaro (the commander) and these four warriors join a big battalion of Japanese soldiers (all forms of cuddly creatures, though many are rabbits) to build an air base there.

The film depicts cuteness, friendliness, and the open-mindedness of the Japanese people and culture because even as the characters built the air base, they taught the natives of the island how to read and write Japanese. The next part of the film is where Momotaro and his battalion of brave soldiers attack another island which is under the control of the British.

The government seemingly created this propaganda film as a last-minute attempt to revive nationalism in the country despite being aware that Japan was losing the war. Although the movie did not find a big audience in 1945, its recovery (it was thought to be destroyed) in 1983 helped rekindle the interest of world cinema in the bunka eiga genre of films. Moreover, *Divine Sea Warriors* is considered to be the first anime feature film ever made.

Another film made during WWII and became popular was *The War at Sea from Hawaii to Malaya* directed by Kajiro Yamamoto. The special effects director, Eiji Tsuburaya, used a miniature set of the Pearl Harbor in the film.

On December 1, 1947, Japan attacked Pearl Harbor triggering the entrance of the US into WWII. After nearly four more years of fighting, the ultimate WWII violent action was the atomic bombings on Hiroshima and Nagasaki in August 1945, which was also the trigger for the end of WWII.

Unfortunately, many factors contributed to the decline of the Japanese cinema industry during WWII. These factors included a weak economy, rising unemployment, and some people also attribute the undue governmental interference to this sorry state at that time. Most of the films at this time in the Japanese film industry were made on the subject of WWII, and many of these were propaganda films.

Japanese Cinema during the American Occupation

After the surrender of Japan to the US in 1945, General Douglas MacArthur was chosen to demilitarize Japan and revise its constitution. The Meiji Constitution was abolished at this time which heralded the end of the Empire of Japan. The country adopted the Constitution of Japan on May 3, 1947.

Now, the Americans believed it was time to turn tables and undo the work of the propaganda spread by Japanese films made during WWII. General MacArthur initiated an 'enlightenment campaign' in which over 600 American movies were distributed and screened all over Japan. The American campaign's goal was to show the US as the cultural, social, and political model in Japan. Nearly all the American films were big commercial successes, and Japan became an important market for American cinema.

However, the American military was suppressing and censoring Japanese films. Only the American versions were allowed to be broadcast, and all other views were banned. The intermingling of Japanese and American art, and especially cinema, has a valid and explicable starting point here with General Douglas MacArthur and W. Edward Deming.

As part of the Japanese reconstruction efforts, General MacArthur took the help of W. Edward Deming who participated in multiple tasks including the 1951 Japanese census and quality control techniques in many government departments. Deming trained scholars, engineers, and managers in quality control and statistical process controls.

The name of Deming, though seemingly irrelevant is an important contributor, (perhaps, unwittingly), to the growth of Japanese cinema. Akio Morita was one of his trainees. Akio Morita is the co-founder of Sony, the Japanese electronics giant, which needs no introduction.

Deming's principle on the importance of maintaining quality for long-term reduced costs and improved productivity and greater market share was learned very well by his trainees including Akio Morita. Nearly all Japanese manufacturers apply Deming's principles to create masterpieces in movies, TV shows, electronic goods, and all other industrial segments. This perfectionist attitude towards quality control is what Japan is known for today. It holds good for filmmaking too.

Akira Kurosawa

A discussion on Japanese films cannot take place without talking about its world-famous director, Akira Kurosawa. He witnessed a large part of the Japanese film journey discussed in the pre-, during, and post-WWII era.

Akira Kurosawa was born in 1910 and revolutionized not only Japanese filmmaking but the global film scene as well. Akira was the youngest of eight children born to a family that descended from an erstwhile samurai family. Akira's family could reportedly trace their samurai family connection to Abe no Sadato, a celebrated warlord in the 11th century.

Akira's father was a director at the Army's school of physical education, and so, the connections of samurai, physical and mental strength, and warfare were deeply etched into Akira's genes and psyche, elements that made him create samurai-based timeless masterpieces.

Akira's father was a very progressive man and urged his family to accept all Western things and thoughts, especially films. Akira saw a lot of movies right from the age of six. His favorite film companion was his brother, Heigo, who was the first person from the Kurosawa family to take up employment in the Japanese film industry.

Remember the benshis of the silent film era who were popular in Japan? ,Akira's elder brother, Heigo Kurosawa, was a celebrated benshi in Tokyo. Heigo was in the film industry and Akira was a painter at that time.

During the 1930s, silent films were on a decline, and like other benshis, Heigo's job opportunities reduced, and he did not have sufficient work. Overcome by depression, he committed suicide in July 1933. The death of his talented elder brother had a big impact on Akira's life. He even spoke about this unfortunate yet unforgettable difficult time of his life in his autobiography. His brother's suicide and another incident in young Akira's life significantly impacted the way he made movies later on in his life.

The other incident took place in 1923 when Tokyo was devastated by the Great Kanto Earthquake. Although Akira and his family were unhurt, Heigo took Akira to see the aftermath of the devastating earthquake. Baseless rumors made the rounds claiming the Koreans were on a looting rampage, which, in turn, triggered multiple attacks on innocent foreigners including Koreans.

The xenophobia created by the rumors left hundreds dead, and Akira saw the blood, gore, and destruction caused directly and indirectly by earthquakes. Heigo forced him to look at the damage even though little Akira wanted to run away from there.

Heigo taught him the importance of facing unpleasant truths without flinching, and this idea greatly influenced his filmmaking style. He was able to depict unpleasant truths in his films boldly and without fear.

A couple of years after his brother's suicide, Akira quit as a painter and entered the Japanese film industry. He worked at Photo Chemical Laboratories (PCL), a new studio at that time. However, later on, PCL became Toho, one of the biggest Japanese studios. At PCL, Akira found his mentor, Kajiro Yamamoto. His talent and his hard work helped Akira rise quickly in the ranks, and soon he became an assistant director on many of Yamamoto's films.

Among the many things he learned under Yamamoto, the most important lesson that catapulted him to world fame was that a good director should also be an excellent screenwriter. He learned and mastered the art of screenwriting and was a co-writer in all of his future films.

Kurosawa and his connection to Samurai

Then, in 1942, Tsuneo Tomita published a judo novel, which Kurosawa read in one sitting, and convinced Toho to buy the filmmaking rights from the author. Toho managed to sign the deal with the author and in 1943, Kurosawa made his directorial debut with the action film, *Sanshiro Sugata*, based on this book.

Getting the film released was not easy as the censor board thought it too Western for Japanese audience sensibilities. A famous director of that time, Yasujiro Ozu, championed Kurosawa's cause, and the film was finally released. The film met with huge commercial success, and soon, Kurosawa was driven to make a sequel called *Zoku Sanshiro Sugata*. As it was made as a propagandist film, *Zoku Sanshiro Sugata* is today considered to be the worst in Kurosawa's film listings.

In 1945, with an intention to make a censor-friendly film, Kurosawa produced *The Men Who Tread on the Tiger's Tail* based on *Kanjincho*, a kabuki play. This film, however, was not completed until 1945, by which time the American occupation of Japan had begun. Now, the American censors banned this film because it was too feudal to suit the modern Japanese tastes. Interestingly, when the film was being made, the Japanese censors (who were in power then) had opined that the content was too Western to suit Japanese sensibilities! This film was finally released in 1952.

In 1948, Kurosawa directed *Drunken Angel* casting a completely unknown actor, Toshiro Mifune. Despite multiple forced censorships, Kurosawa claimed that this was the first film where he was given complete creative freedom. Mifune's performance earned him huge critical acclaim, and the Kurosawa-Mifune duo went on to make many more films.

The year 1950 is considered to be the birth of the Golden Age of Japanese Cinema because, in that year, Kurosawa made the incredible film, *Rashomon,* and released it to the cinema lovers of the world, in general, and Japan in particular. Although it was only a moderate success in Japan when it was released for the first time, *Rashomon* was chosen for the Venice Film Festival, even as Kurosawa started work on his next venture.

In September 1951, *Rashomon* got Venice Film Festival's most illustrious award, the Golden Lion. This movie showcased Kurosawa's directorial skills in unprecedented ways. He was able to combine the essence of American pulp fiction, Western filmmaking skills and techniques, traditional Eastern culture, and Shakespeare's story-telling skills to produce a string of masterpieces that revolutionized Japanese and world cinema.

He was able to break away from well-known yet traditional Japanese film content and styles of Mizoguchi and Ozu, and create a new exclusive niche for himself. *Rashomon* broke geographical barriers, gave Kurosawa international credence as a legendary director, and set the pace for the Golden Age of Japanese Cinema, which, experts believe, lasted for an entire decade.

Hollywood Films Inspired by Kurosawa

There are many remakes of Kurosawa's films. It would be unfair not to talk about the one movie that impacted Hollywood and other film industries significantly, the *Seven Samurai*.

Seven Samurai (SS) – One of the most thrilling movies of all times, Akira Kurosawa's Seven Samurai (1954), Shichinin no samurai in Japanese, follows the tale of a 16th-century village hounded by a gang of invading bandits. The villagers are at their wit's end because of the marauding bandits and hire seven samurai warriors for protection.

The period of the film is 1586, a difficult time in Japanese history. Numerous conflicts between the nobles of different regions in the country existed, and the poor peasant is caught in the middle of these conflicts even as he struggles to live simply and peacefully in the chaotic world. The samurai at that time had also become wandering warriors and ronins (without a master). The nobles feared the ronins' fighting powers and strengths and were always trying to hunt them down.

The film begins with the news of an upcoming bandit attack on a poor mountainside village which has just harvested its barley. One of the village elders decides that the best way to protect their new harvest from these bandits is to hire samurai warriors. The villagers point out an obvious fact to the old man. They say, "We have nothing to pay them except rice." To this, the wise old man answers, "Then, find hungry samurai." This dialogue has taken proportions of folklore among Kurosawa fans.

The antagonist in *Seven Samurai* does not have excessive depth in character. Experts believe that this approach makes it easy for the audience to enjoy the agonies he suffers at the hands of the protagonists. There is nothing human about the antagonists. They don't need a reason to plunder and kill.

The urge for destruction is simply a force of nature with them making the impending danger and threat from such antagonists even more terrifying. The villagers know that the raids will continue until every bandit is killed or the village is completely razed to the ground and there is nothing left to raid.

The clientele in SS is represented by Rikichi, a ferocious man from the affected village who is ready to do anything to fight back against the bandits. He is supported ably by the village elder which angers the other villagers who prefer to take a less aggressive approach to the problem.

In addition to losing his grains to the bandits, Rikichi's wife was also taken away to become their sex slave. The audience realizes the second aspect of Rikichi's character only later on in the film, and almost immediately can connect to his deep anguish and anger against the bandits.

The leader of the Seven Samurai is Kambei Shimada. When Rikichi and his friends from the village first see him, they find him cutting off his top-knot, a ceremonially critical element for any samurai. And in those times, status meant a lot. However, Kambei was willing to make this sacrifice so that he could disguise himself as a monk to save a kidnapped child from a thief holed up in the barn. The scene of cutting off his top-knot reflects the protagonist's selfless humility and compassion to save the innocent from evil. Rikichi realizes he has found the village's savior.

This 3-hour film weaves a seamless tapestry through philosophy, entertainment, human emotions, and of course, amazing samurai action. The story is an unforgettable tale of hope and courage.

The Magnificent Seven - Now, come to *The Magnificent Seven* (MS) made in the US only six years after the release of the *Seven Samurai*. Directed by John Sturge, *The Magnificent Seven* (1960), is a classic American western genre film and a faithfully rendered remake of *Seven Samurai*. John Sturge leaves the plot almost intact and changes only the tropes of samurai into those of the American West.

The period in which the *Magnificent Seven* was set is unclear. However, there is little doubt in the minds of the viewers that it was around the end of the 'Old West,' which is similar to the setting of <u>*Seven Samurai*</u>. The story of *Magnificent Seven* is set in a village bordering between the US and Mexico where bandits keep creating problems for the innocent villagers.

The bandits take goods and food and shoot down any villager who tried to protest, thereby instilling fear in the rest of the villagers who dumbly hand over their share. The leader of the bandits tells the villagers that they can expect more such raids. Here too, an elderly villager comes forward and advises his people to hire gunslingers (instead of samurai warriors) from the neighboring town for protection.

In MS, the antagonist has a more humanizing aspect to him. He hugs his victims before robbing from them and talks like how a father would talk to his children, funny and almost loving. Yet, the dangerous undertones are unmistakable. A favorite dialogue reflecting his 'danger-laced' fatherly attitude is, "If God didn't want them sheared, why did he make them sheep?"

The clientele is MS is also represented by a Rikichi-like character, Hilario, who also gets support from the village elder to find gunslingers. A primary difference between Hilario of MS and Rikichi of SS is that there is no wife-related story for the former, which, in some ways, reduces the depth of his character, unlike that of Rikichi.

In MS, the leader of the protagonist team is Chris Larabee Adams. When Hilario and his friends first find him, he is volunteering to bury a slain Native American in the graveyard of the town, which is a forbidden act in those times, when Native Americans were discriminated against. As the funeral procession moves forward, Chris efficiently disarms and subdues the town protestors winning the heart of Hilario and his friends immediately.

Here is a list of other Kurosawa movies that impacted film industries across the world including Hollywood:

- *Yojimbo* remade as *Fist of Dollars* (1964) and *Last Man Standing* (1996) - Hollywood
- *Rashomon* remade as *The Outrage* - Hollywood

- *Seven Samurai* remade as *Seven Warriors* – Hong Kong
- *Rashomon* remade as *U-Mong Pa Meung* (2011) - Thailand

Many other films and TV series have been inspired by Kurosawa. Unfortunately not all of them give credit for the inspiration. But, that doesn't stop true cinema lovers to find the unmistakable Kurosawa connection even in these films.

The legend has left an indelible mark that will not be forgotten for a long, long time to come. As world lovers of art and cinema, we must pay homage to this amazingly outstanding filmmaker who set new standards in filmmaking and story-telling.

Hayao Miyazaki and the Impact of His Movies on the Western World

Hayao Miyazaki is a famous and highly acclaimed Japanese director whose animated films have revolutionized the children's film genre. His childhood in Tokyo was spent amidst the bombings and ravages of WWII. His well-to-do family, fortunately, survived the war. However, the effects of the war, the Pacifist attitude relevant at that time, and the continuous man-nature conflict left deep scars in Miyazaki's psyche.

The effects of his exposure to WWII and the struggle of Japan after the war, perhaps, led Miyazaki to live life at the edge, dangling between the worlds of adult reality and childhood fantasy. These childhood scars are clearly reflected in all his animated movies, which strive to retain the emotional earnestness and reverence largely witnessed in the world of children, which is the reason for the huge impact of his animated films on the western world.

Why choose animation? A large part of his childhood took place in post-war Japan in which Osamu Tezuka, the father of manga, revolutionized the world of Japanese comics. He read these comics multiple times and fell in love with them, and from then, Miyazaki's dream was to become a comic artist.

In college, however, he studied economics and political science even though his love for manga and dream of becoming a comic artist were still alive and kicking. He pursued his passion for comics in college by setting up a manga club even as he mastered economics and political science.

The trigger for the turn to animation came in the form of the first color anime feature film called *The Tale of the White Serpent (Hakujaden)* produced by Toei Animation Studios in 1958 when Miyazaki was a high school teenager. This Chinese folk story featured a young boy who loves a snake goddess in human form. The film had a profound impact on this young boy so much so that he watched the movie many times over.

He said later on that he had also fallen in love with the human snake goddess, Bai-Nang, and also admitted in a 1979 essay that he turned to animation because of *Hakujaden*. When he watched this movie, he stated it was as if 'the scales from my eyes had fallen' and he felt that with animation, he will be able to portray the innocence and honesty of children.

The Golden Age of Japanese Cinema

Kurosawa started with *Rashomon*; but, continued for a long, long time after that creating masterpiece after masterpiece, enticing and inspiring the world. Kurosawa's other works that influenced an entire generation of new filmmakers in the world include:

- *Seven Samurai*
- *Throne of Blood (an adaptation of Macbeth)*
- *The Hidden Fortress*
- *Yojimbo*
- *Red Beard*

All of these films achieved international success and critical acclaim changing the way filmmakers made films.

Moreover, Japanese filmdom as a whole was finding new, innovative ways to depict the realities going on around them. In 1954, nuclear tests were conducted in the Pacific Ocean off the coast of the Japanese islands resulting in radioactive storms in the mainland.

A fishing vessel fell victim to these tests and created a heightened state of panic in Japan which was still struggling with the brutality caused by the Nagasaki and Hiroshima bombings. Many Japanese directors, including Kurosawa, focused on the fallouts from these nuclear tests under a completely different genre.

Again, under Toho's banner, Japan created its biggest movie superstar, Godzilla, alternatively transliterated as "Gojira" in Japanese. Directed by Ishiro Honda, *Godzilla* used the allegory of the atomic bombings. Honda had filmed multiple documentary footages of war-torn Tokyo, and his friend, Akira Kurosawa used some of them in his film, *Stray Dog*.

Godzilla also had another special effect superstar, Eiji Tsuburaya, the technical film expert responsible for creating the miniature model of Pearl Harbor for *The War at Sea from Hawaii to Malaya* directed by Yamamoto during WWII. In 1954, Toho produced two huge blockbusters simultaneously, Ishiro Honda's *Godzilla* and Kurosawa's *Seven Samurai*, nearly driving the studio to bankruptcy.

Both the films of 1954 received Best Film nominations from Japanese Academy Awards. Seven Samurai walked away with the honors. During the Golden Age, Yasujiro Ozu created his masterpiece, *Tokyo Story*, one of the best movies ever made.

Moreover, foreign awards tumbled in for Japanese cinema during this period. Some of the great Japanese films and the awards they won include:

- Hiroshi Inagaki's film Samurai I: *Musashi Miyamoto* - won the Oscars for the Best Foreign Language Film.
- Hiroshi Inagaki's film *The Rickshaw Man* won the Golden Lion.
- Kon Ichikawa's movie *The Burmese Harp* was nominated for the Best Foreign Language Film.
- Kenji Mizoguchi's movie *Ugetsu* won the Silver Bear.

Horror Films in Japan

The concept of horror in Japan can be traced to a multitude of folklore stories that describes ghosts and spirits and their desire for revenge and retribution. These horror folk stories are referred to as yokai, or ghost stories, and have been passed on through generations orally.

Interestingly, Lafcadio Hearn, an Irish folklorist who was one of the very few foreigners to integrate into the Japanese society completely and seamlessly, was the man responsible for writing down these yokai stories for the first time. His collection of yokai tales was published in 1904 and was titled *Kwaidan: Stories and Studies of Strange Things.*

Yet, the genre of horror films in Japan (except for a very few old ones that are not extant) started very late in Japan, in 1964 to be precise. *Onibaba*, directed by Kaneto Shindo, released in 1964, is considered to be the first Japanese horror film. In 1965, Masaki Kobayashi released the film, *Kwaidan*, which was a selection of yokai stories from Hearn's anthology.

Kwaidan won the Special Jury Prize at the Cannes Film Festival of that year catapulting the movie and its director to international fame. Kobayashi influenced many other horror film directors in Japan and other countries. His approach to horror was an unrelenting sense of dread throughout the film that climaxed at the end.

This approach was very different from the prevailing horror films in America, which used jump-scare tactics in the form of sudden reactions accompanied by loud noises to create horror and fear. Kobayashi approached the horror genre through psychology wherein the fear for the audience came from what was not shown on the screen. This method ensured that the film stayed in the minds of the audience for a long time after the movie ended.

Following *Kwaidan*, masterpieces in horror film genre from Japan did not happen until 1977 when Nobuhiko Obayashi made *Hausu*, a combination of horror and comedy that was well-accepted by cinema goers around the world. The story is of a young girl who brings a set of friends to visit her aunt who is a vampire feeding on the blood of young girls to remain youthful. The technical experimentation done in *Hausu* created a surreal environment which inspired generations of Japanese and foreign directors.

Japanese horror films didn't achieve its own name until the 1990s and were collectively referred to as J-Horror. Some great horror films made during this time include:

- ***Ringu (1998) by Hideo Nakata*** – remade in America as The Ring in 2002. Using the psychological dread inspired by Kobayashi, Ringu gripped the Japanese and the US audience in its horror-filled grasp.
- ***Pulse (2001) by Kiyoshi Kurosawa*** – included horror as well as contemporary social issues; inspired by the fear of Y2K, Pulse depicts a yokai (Japanese folklore term for ghosts) taking control of the internet inflicting psychological and physical trauma on its victims
- ***Ju-on; The Grudge (2002) by Takashi Shimizu*** – was based on Japanese folklore and depicted the spirits of a woman and her child taking control of and haunting the house in which they were murdered. This movie was remade in America in 2004.

Combining satire, comedy, and special effects aesthetics, the directors of J-Horror continue to push limits in this genre and bring out some amazing masterpieces that grip the world's imagination. Other Japanese horror films that are extremely popular include Yoshihiro Nishimura's *Tokyo Gore Police* (2008), *Vampire Girl vs. Frankenstein Girl* (2009), and *Mutant Girls Squad* (2010), Hideo Nakata's *Dark Water* (2002), and Noboru Iguchi's *The Machine Girl* (2008) and *Dead Sushi* (2012).

Interestingly, the Japanese horror film genre continues to be inspired by its folklore and yokai stories, and Kwaidan has an impact even today on the making of horror films in Japan and the world over.

How Japanese Films Influenced Hollywood Films

The outstanding movies made by exceptional Japanese directors inspired an entire brood of renowned Hollywood directors for the next half-century. Many western directors credited Japanese classics to have influenced their projects directly. Additionally, Deming's principle of quality control, which gave rise to multiple Japanese conglomerates such as Toyota and Sony, was now replicated in America.

The assembly line operations from these Japanese giants were copied by **Ed Catmull,** the President of Disney Animation and Pixar Animation. He said the flexibility and freedom given to individual employees on the assembly line to raise concerns and give feedback was a culture that drove the early success of Pixar Animation.

Hollywood directors were almost obsessed by Akira Kurosawa's films and adapted many of them as cowboy Western genre movies. Director Sergio Leone remade Kurosawa's works to such levels of similarity that every frame of the Hollywood adaptation matched with the original Japanese one. Some of them include:

- *Seven Samurai* was adapted as *The Magnificent Seven*
- *Yojimbo* became *A Fistful of Dollars*
- *Star Wars* was highly influenced by *The Hidden Fortress*

Martin Scorsese and Steven Spielberg called Kurosawa their sensei, the Japanese term for role model and teacher. Spielberg said of Kurosawa, "I have learned the most from him than from anyone else on this planet." And Scorsese said, "Akira was not my master but the master of generations of filmmakers."

Why Godzilla continues to be at the Top of Japanese Pop Culture

For those who haven't seen Godzilla (the 1954 original version), here is a prophetic message from Kyohei Yamane (the archeologist character in the film). At the end of the film, he declares that if countries do not stop their nuclear testing programs, then Godzilla will reappear in another part of the world.

Godzilla didn't just come back once, but repeatedly across the world including from Hollywood directors. The different governments of the world continue their nuclear testing, and Toho Company continues to create new installments of Godzilla. The Godzilla franchise holds the cinema-going audience in awe as the monster keeps appearing in over thirty sequels since 1954. The modern-day Godzilla fights against dragons as well as extraterrestrial cyborgs from outer space.

Let us start with the birth of this monster in the hands of Ishiro Honda, confidante and friend of Akira Kurosawa, in 1954. This movie was a stark portrait of the horrors of WWII and reflected the fear of the Japanese nation in the aftermath of the Nagasaki and Hiroshima bombings.

Within six months of the first franchise's release, the flexibility of this monster-hero character was evident. In 1955, the second sequel in the franchise was *Godzilla Raids Again* in which our favorite superstar monster battles a gargantuan irradiated Ankylosaurus.

Godzilla made its debut in America with the top actor of those times, Raymond Burr, playing the lead role, in 1956. The title of the American Godzilla was, *Godzilla, King of the Monsters.*

Despite Honda's attempts not to convert his monster born out of a nuclear accident into a spectator sport, he and Jun Fukuda, the franchise partner for a long time, churned out 15 installments of the movie by 1975. Haruo Nakajima played the role of Godzilla in more than 12 films, more than any other Godzilla actor. He suffered innumerable injuries including electric shocks, burns, and even near death due to suffocation.

Here is a list of Godzilla movies produced by the Toho Company:

- 1954 - *Godzilla (Godzilla, King of The Monsters)*
- 1955 - *Godzilla Raids Again*
- 1962 - *King Kong vs. Godzilla*
- 1964 - *Mothra vs. Godzilla*
- 1964 - *Ghidorah, the Three-Headed Monster*

- 1965 - *Invasion of Astro-Monster (Godzilla vs. Monster Zero)*
- 1966 - *Ebirah, Horror of the Deep (Godzilla vs. the Sea Monster)*
- 1967 - *Son of Godzilla*
- 1968 - *Destroy All Monsters*
- 1969 - *All Monsters Attack (Godzilla's Revenge)*
- 1971 - *Godzilla vs. Hedorah (Godzilla vs. the Smog Monster)*
- 1972 - *Godzilla vs. Gigan*
- 1973 - *Godzilla vs. Megalon*
- 1974 - *Godzilla vs. Mechagodzilla*
- 1975 - *Terror of Mechagodzilla*
- 1984 - *The Return of Godzilla (Godzilla 1985)*
- 1989 - *Godzilla vs. Biollante*
- 1991 - *Godzilla vs. King Ghidorah*
- 1992 - *Godzilla vs. Mothra (Godzilla & Mothra: The Battle for Earth)*
- 1993 - *Godzilla vs. Mechagodzilla II*
- 1994 - *Godzilla vs. SpaceGodzilla*
- 1995 - *Godzilla vs. Destoroyah*
- 1999 - *Godzilla 2000: Millennium (Godzilla 2000)*
- 2000 - *Godzilla vs. Megaguirus*
- 2001 - *Godzilla, Mothra and King Ghidorah: Giant Monsters All-Out Attack*
- 2002 - *Godzilla Against Mechagodzilla*
- 2003 - *Godzilla: Tokyo S.O.S.*
- 2004 - *Godzilla: Final Wars*
- 2007 - *Always: Sunset on Third Street 2*

- 2016 - *Godzilla Resurgence (Shin Godzilla)*
- 2017 - *Godzilla: Planet of the Monsters*
- 2018 - *Godzilla: City on the Edge of Battle*

Godzilla was continuously packaged in new formats with relevant inclusions of each decade/period to retain and rekindle audience interest. After the 1975 installment, Toho put Godzilla into hibernation. However, our friendly, and sometimes, goofy monster found his way into American comics.

Through various twists, turns, and repackages (some installments meeting with failures too), Godzilla in 2014 appeared again, perhaps, thanks to a revival of superheroes in cinemas. The design of the MUTO (short of Massive Unknown Terrestrial Creature), the primary antagonist in the latest version, was inspired by multiple characters including *King Kong, Jurassic Park,* and *Starship Troopers.* The Godzilla of 1998 and another one in 2014 were entirely under Hollywood production banners. The rest are all under the Toho banner.

The tsunami of 2011 that left Japan completely battered including a nuclear meltdown at the Fukushima power plants was featured in the 2016 Shin Godzilla version, the first Godzilla movie that was made under the Toho production banner after nearly a decade. There were three more anime versions made in 2017 and 2018 as well.

Godzilla has become too huge to disappear completely even if the franchise's success rates go up and down. The western world, in particular, and the entire globe, in general will continue its nuclear testing capabilities and bring Godzilla back repeatedly to suit the sensibilities of each new generation by infusing the features of manmade and natural catastrophes encountered by every generation. Ishiro Honda can rest in peace knowing he has created a monster that mankind will take a very long time to forget.

Impact of Japanese Animation Films on Hollywood

Giant Ghibli clock on facade of Nittele Tower
in Shiodome area, Minato

Hayao Miyazaki set up his Ghibli Studio in 1985, and the first movie that rolled out from here was *Castle in the Sky*. His biggest hit was *Spirited Away* released in 2000. This movie, distributed in America by Disney, went on to gain immense success and huge popularity.

The lessons learned by American animation (unheard of until then) from Hayao Miyazaki, and later incorporated successfully into stunning movies like *Frozen* and *Brave* include:

- Use of *computer graphics was limited; Miyazaki was a purist and believed in hand-drawing his animations right to the last intricate detail.*
- *For the 1997 hit movie, Princess Mononoke, Miyazaki himself drew and revised over 80,000 frames; critics claim that this detailed and purist approach to animations are the reasons for his movies' engrossing visual style.*
- *The scripting was invariably organically done alongside the animation and production. Therefore, the story unfolded even as the animation progressed. This approach is the reason for the honest and deeply personal touch in each of his masterpieces.*
- *Scripting was never done before animation which is another unique feature of Miyazaki, and now followed by Western animators too.*
- *Both Frozen and Brave follow the theme of intrepid young girls, another key feature lifted from Spirited Away which told the story of a 10-year-old girl, Chihiro, who rescues her parents from a witch's magic spell. Even if the stories of young brave girls reflect the prevailing shift towards gender equality in the present times, many American animators and filmmakers credit Miyazaki for this change in perspective.*

Important Japanese Film Studios

Films cannot be made without films studios, and so here is a brief historical overview of the major Japanese film studios.

Daiei – This studio happily provided propaganda films during WWII. However, after the war, it lost its impact following the imposition by the Americans on the jidaigeki genre of films. However, some great films continued to come out from its stables; the most famous one being Kurosawa's Rashomon in 1951. The studio also produced Mizoguchi's The Life of O'Haru in 1952. The 1954 color movie from Daiei, The Gates of Hell, achieved commercial success in foreign countries, which sustained the company, but then went into decline during the 1960s and shut shop in 1971.

Kadokawa – Starting off as a publishing house in 1945, Kadokawa ventured into film production in 1976. This studio has a large library of movies not originally produced by itself but owns other film-making companies such as Asmik Ace and Daiei (which it acquired in 2002). So, many of the titles have been rebranded under Kadokawa umbrella.

However, in the 1990s, it made an impact on the film industry of Europe and America through the production of masterpieces such as *Dark Water* and *Ringu* both directed by Hideo Nakata.

Nikkatsu – An abbreviation for Nippon Katsudō Shashin, Nikkatsu is one of the oldest Japanese film studios, founded way back in 1912. However, it lost out on film business in the 1940s because of wartime controls. The studio was not able to make a film until 1954 after which there was a spawning of yakuza (Japanese term for gangster) films, mostly featuring Suzuki Seijun; the famous yakuza actor, filmmaker, and director.

PCL and Toho – PCL or Photo Chemical Laboratory was the precursor of Toho. Kobayashi Ichizo purchased this small production company (Kurosawa's first employer) in 1936 to set up the foundation for the Toho Group. Toho had a long, bittersweet relationship with Akira Kurosawa and produced some brilliant movies all along the difficult, but worthwhile, relationship. Toho is famous in Japan as well as in Europe and the US, thanks to its sci-fi, samurai, and Godzilla films. Toho also distributed Miyazaki's animated films from Studio Ghibli.

Toei Studios – is the production house that made Miyazaki's childhood favorite anime feature film, *The Tale of the White Serpent (Hakujaden)*. During the 1940s, Disney Studios was already making super hit feature films such as *Fantasia* and

Pinocchio in 1940 and *Bambi* in 1942. These movies aroused a lot of interest in the Japanese film industry, and were especially important to Toei Studios.

Toei Studios set up a committee to study and research cartoons, which expressed doubts about Japan's ability to make cartoons to match Hollywood standards. Despite these apprehensions, Toei Studios bought a small independent studio called Nichi Dôeiga and created its own self-sufficient animation studio, called Toei Doga.

Initially, it started making television advertisements to increase revenue, sent its staff to the US to be trained under the experts there, and then developed its own style of manga-based cartoons. After a series of short films titled *Kitten's Doodling (Koneko no rakugaki)*, Toei created *The Legend of the White Snake (Hakujaden)* in 1958 which earned commercial success and critical acclaim.

This movie was also exported to other countries including the US, Hong Kong, Taiwan, and Brazil even though Disney continued its dominance on animation cinema. Since then, though various ups and downs in their business, Toei Animation continues to contribute to world animation.

Some of the most favorite shows from Toei Animation that are still popular around the globe include World Trigger, Kyousou Giga, Yu-Gi-Oh! Interstella5555: The Story of the secret Star System, Digimon Adventures, Dragon Ball Super, Bishoujo Senshi Sailor Moon, One Piece, and many more.

Summarily, films, film studios, directors, and other critical members from the Japanese film industry have learned from and contributed to world cinema in a mind-boggling number of ways. The happiest thing about this intermingling of great cultures is that the common citizen of the world gets to experience the resonating effects of the mergers. We must thank these great people in Japan and the western world for the excellent interchange of creative and business ideas.

Chapter 2:
Japanese TV Shows

Many Japanese TV shows have their origins in role-playing video games (RPGs). The popularity of the games drove the promoters to other media outlets to increase profits and build their customer base. So, most of them transferred game characters to trading cards to TV shows to anime, and even to movies. TV shows such as *Pokémon* are more popular in the US than many of the home-based shows.

Let us look at the origins and popularity of some of these TV shows that broke geographical borders in unprecedented ways.

Pokémon

The Pokémon TV show is one of the most successful and longest-running TV shows in the history of TV shows. But before we go to the TV show, let us start when the concept of Pokémon began in the minds of the creators, Satoshi Tajiri and his friend, Ken Sugimori.

Created by Satoshi Tajiri, Pokémon is an abbreviation for 'Pocket Monsters'. As a child, he loved to collect tadpoles and insects, and it was this passion that gave him the idea to create *Pokémon*. When he first saw the Game Boy device along with its Link Cable, he envisioned insects crawling along the cable.

As a child, Satoshi Tajiri loved a TV show called *Ultra Seven* in which giant monsters were encapsulated in small containers. His love for insect collection and the monsters of

Ultra Seven held in small capsules gave Satoshi the idea for *Pokémon*. In fact, the first iteration of *Pokémon* was called Capsule Monsters.

In the early 1980s, Satoshi Tajiri and Ken Sugimori started a magazine called *Game Freak* in which these Capsule Monsters appeared. Satoshi was the writer and Sugimori was the illustrator. However, this duo realized that the arcade gaming scene seemed to be declining and decided to develop new games under the umbrella of Game Freak. The games they developed during that time included:

- Games for NES Nintendo
- Yoshi on Game Boy
- Magical Tarurūto-Kun on SEGA's Mega Drive

Game Freak's games were also published by Sony back then.

Satoshi and his friend approached Nintendo with the Pokémon idea. Initially, Nintendo was not very keen on it, and Satoshi and Co had to fund the project themselves. While Satoshi handled the idea part, Sugimori worked on the artwork, and another colleague, Junichi Masuda worked on the music and sound effects. In fact, before Nintendo finally decided to support Satoshi, Game Freak almost went bankrupt investing all its resources on the Pokémon project.

Despite initial misgivings, about the idea, Nintendo decided to give the benefit of the doubt to Tajiri and Co and decided to fund the Pokémon project and publish the games on its consoles. The first games called Pokémon Red and Green were released for Game Boy on February 27, 1996. In these versions (which had 151 Pokémon), players were allowed to capture, train, and trade their Pokémon to achieve the ultimate result of becoming a Pokémon Master.

The initial sales were quite modest. However, after an event centered on the legendary Pokémon, Mew, the sales improved rapidly, and Pokémon Blue was also released which featured more features and better visuals than Red and Green.

At the very core, Pokémon was a role-playing video game (RPG) that allowed players to play the role of Pokémon trainers, traveling through the world to collect miniature monsters and train them to battle other Pokémon. The concept of collecting miniature monsters was inspired by Satoshi's insect-collecting hobby as a child.

Every generation of kids got hooked to the ferocious yet lovable Pokémon. Their demand for new ones spearheaded the creation of more miniature monsters, and today the Pokémon count is more than 700! Once the game achieved immense popularity, it was time to increase profits by creating trading cards first, and the *Pokémon* TV show, second.

The first *Pokémon* TV show was aired on April 1, 1997, in Japan. The main protagonist in the TV show was Ash Ketchum (the tagline of the series was 'gotta catch 'em all') who was Pokémon Red, and his rival was Gary Oak, who was Pokémon Blue. The TV show garnered popularity rapidly, and the anime followed too.

The TV show depicts 10-year-old Ketchum starting his Pokémon collection journey which is fraught with challenges including not getting any of the three best Pokémon from his mentor and teacher (he was late, and the three best were given away to other trainers), Professor Oak. He had to be content with a Pokémon that nobody wanted and was lying around, the headstrong and troublesome Pikachu.

Thus, began the journey of Ketchum and Pikachu as they traveled the world, collecting Pokémon regularly, and overcoming various challenges in every episode. The TV show was released in North America in September 1998, and achieved immense success very rapidly which resulted in the first Pokémon movie titled *Mewtwo Strikes Back*. In the US, this movie briefly held the highest opening gross collections for an animation.

The TV show became so popular across the world that ironically, some of the game features were copied from the episodes. So, there were new Pokémon games released that were titled Special Pikachu Edition, and Ketchum TV show adventures found their way into the new games.

Reasons for Pokémon Popularity

Why did Pokémon achieve such immense popularity not only in its birth country but also across the world including among the high-demanding western world consumers? Here are some answers:

Cross-Media Entity – Pokémon was not just a TV show; it was a cultural phenomenon spanning games, comics, trading cards, TV shows, anime, and movies. Whichever medium you like, you will find an outstanding Pokémon version perfectly tuned to that particular medium. This multiple-pronged approach captured a wide range of audiences.

Brought Many Communities Together – This series was never about allowing players to sort out their problems on their own. The promoters and owners always organized events in which players met and interacted with each other and Pokémon characters thereby increasing community engagement. Fans and idols were constantly in touch through these regular Pokémon events held at different places.

Serialized TV Shows- Starting with Ash receiving his first Pokémon (the abandoned and seemingly troublesome Pikachu), the TV show captures his journey of collecting Pokémon slowly but surely earning his badges, battling villains, and always finding himself a bit behind his rival, Gary Oak.

Each episode can be watched as a stand-alone. Yet, there is some event that binds each episode with its previous and its next one making the TV show appear as one big never-ending epic narrated in a serial form. Every victory of Ash Ketchum was celebrated by his fans, and every defeat was a signal that the story will go on. It was the hooking element.

Pokémon's presentation and heart-touching stories broke all geographical barriers. Ash Ketchum will always remain the 10-year-old Pokémon trainer. His youth and popularity will never fade.

Pokémon and Its Ties to Japanese Mythology

Although Satoshi Tajiri's childhood passion for insect collecting was the primary inspiration, there are deep ties between Pokémon and the ancient Japanese mythology as well. The animist origins and myths of Japan also offer rich inspirations that were happily included into the Pokémon series by Game Freak and Nintendo.

Shintoism is the oldest Japanese religion that is followed even today. Shinto teaches that our world is occupied by numerous kami or gods who can be appeased through offerings of food and incense. When kami are happy and appeased, they will bestow their blessings by giving you success in your business, personal life, health, and studies. However, if the kami are disrespected, they become vindictive. Here are some obvious parallels between Pokémon and kami or gods:

- The Pokémon Whiscash is very similar to namazu, a catfish in Shintoism that can cause earthquakes if displeased.
- The Pokémon Shiftry is a goblin, or tengu, in Japanese mythology.
- Kami, along with the sinister yokai, live in trees, rocks, and other natural habitats. Pokémon also inhabit such places.
- In Pokémon Go, the Pokémon become your friends when you offer food and incense. Like the kami, they shower you

with blessings by rewarding you with special items and extra points.

- If displeased, the Pokémon can escape capture and run away, making you lose points (like the displeased and vindictive kami).

So, religion and beliefs are deeply embedded in Pokémon, and why not? Today, it is true that nearly all religions of the world use advanced technologies to spread and preach their tenets. Japan chooses to use games and TV shows!

Yo-Kai Watch

Yo-Kai Watch is a game and anime. Like Pokémon, Yo-Kai Watch puts players in the shoes of a young boy or girl who controls yokai (or spirits) to play RPG games. The game series from Nintendo became popular enough to spawn an anime TV show, movies, comics, and cards, and toys. Developed by Level-5 (which also developed other popular games such as Inazuma Eleven and Professor Layton), Yo-Kai Watch took some to reach its peak of popularity.

In fact, when the first iteration was released in July 2013, there was a lukewarm response in Japan. However, the anime TV show created and aired in January 2014 ignited sales of the game. The release of Yo-kai Watch 2 in July 2015 took the sales soaring even further. So, what is Yo-Kai Watch based on?

Like Pokémon, Yo-Kai Watch is inspired by Japanese spirits found in the country's folklore. All the characters and settings of the game are based on yokai spirits; though all of them get a cute, modern-day, humorous twist.

In Japanese myth, these yokai could be phantoms or mundane objects or people who have discovered their higher life purposes. Like Pokémon again, Yo-Kai Watch is an RPG where the player chooses to be the girl or boy empowered (with the special watch) to see yokai that are invisible to the naked eye. The yokai like those from Japanese folklore are found everywhere and yet, can be seen only by specially-gifted people.

Nathan "Nate" Adams (the boy character) is an 11-year-old boy who is an average student. Despite his mediocrity, Nate is an active, fun-loving, and a popular boy is in class. Once when he was roaming in the forest, he freed Whisper, a friendly yokai, who gifted him a watch with which Nate can 'see and capture' other yokai, and use their powers to do good things for the world.

The female protagonist is Katie Forester, Nate classmate. She is intelligent and is adored by many of her male classmates including Nate. However, she always worries that she is falling short of her mother's expectations. Katie also has a Yo-Kai which she wears around her neck.

The Yo-Kai characters in the game and the anime series are Whisper (Nate's self-appointed butler), Jibanyan (a cat yokai), Komasan (lion dog yokai), Usapyon (a shady yokai from America), and many more.

So, did Yo-Kai Watch try and emulate Pokémon? Well, there is little doubt that it did especially regarding the collection of yokai (collecting Pokémon) and the premise and settings based on Japanese folklore. However, the premise was different, and the characters were handled very differently.

The game and TV show debuted in America in 2016. However, it did not reach the same enthusiastic levels as it did in Japan primarily because of the distinctive Japanese feel that many of the Westerners could not relate to. The kids in Japan were able to sense the familiarity *Yo-Kai Watch* offered to them, thanks to the fact that most Japanese families still follow, believe, and teach their children the tenets of Shinto faith.

Moreover, the settings of the TV show and the game have deep Japanese connections because the adventures of Nate and Katie take place in Japanese neighborhoods with a lot of characters from Japanese mythological classics. This approach made the franchise very popular in Japan while not so in the Western world.

Power Rangers

When Americans think of superheroes, the images conjured up are usually those of the Justice League or the Avengers. In Japan, these superheroes don't stand a chance against one or more of the Super Sentai; the masked heroes who immigrated to the US as the Power Rangers.

The *Super Sentai* franchise started in 1975 in Japan as part of a genre called Tokusatsu (or live-action shows) in which movies and TV shows depended heavily on special effects. Tokusatsu in Japanese translates to 'special filming.' The

Tokusatsu genre is fairly wide and covers nearly all special effects shows and films including *Godzilla, Kamen Rider,* and *Super Sentai.*

There are over 40 seasons of *Super Sentai,* which change every year. Each new season, which is usually once a year, brings a new set of actors, hero transformations, and a completely new story. The premise of this superhero tokusatsu TV series is very basic. There is a team of young people (men and women) called Sentai (Japanese for squadron) that comes together to fight against monsters and evil people threatening to destroy the world.

Each superhero has a special battle suit, which he or she wears to access powerful weapons and get superhero abilities. When the Super Sentai wear their costumes, they are empowered to be mightiest heroes on Earth.

Before the Super Sentai migrated to the US as the Power Rangers, a Hollywood element affected them while they were still in Japan. In 1978, Toei struck a deal with Marvel Comics to create a tokusatsu (live action) TV series titled Spider-Man hoping that the deal will result in Marvel Comics getting the rights to Super Sentai for distribution in the US. The Spider-Man series, which had a giant robot called Leopardon as

Spider-Man's right-hand man, lasted only one year after which the Marvel-Toei deal fell through.

However, inspired by the giant robot of Takuya Yamashiro (the civilian identity of the Japanese Spider-Man), every Super Sentai team got its own giant robot to fight evil and protect the world along with the 'super' in their title. Such incidents are reflective of the trading ideas that took place between Japan and the US.

The Adaptation of Super Sentai into Power Rangers

Power Rangers episodes drew heavily on Super Sentai episodes including some frame-by-frame copies of shots. They used footages and plot lines from *Super Sentai* to create new episodes of Power Rangers. This time, Saban Entertainment struck a deal with Toei to air Super Sentai in the US. However, unlike Marvel, Saban Entertainment only wanted to take the action scenes from Super Sentai to use them in an entirely new action series, which they called *Power Rangers*.

This approach was possible because all the action scenes were shot with masked characters, and therefore, they were unrecognizable. Saban Entertainment only needed to change the surrounded content and the premise of the series. Of course, cost-cutting was a big motivation too.

For example, the *Mighty Morphin Power Rangers* Season 1 was Kyoryu Sentai Zyuranger in which Zyuranger from Super Sentai was left out, and the first season of *Power Rangers* with 40 episodes adapted plenty of footage from Super Sentai Season I. Excessively Japanese and violent elements were edited from these footages to lessen the Asian country's effects and to meet the demands of American parents who didn't want excessive violence. Similar adaptations were made to the other *Super Sentai* seasons and episodes for the *Power Rangers* were created for the US audience.

The action was changed to a fictional town in California and the team of Power Rangers consisted of five 'teenagers with attitude.' The witch Bandora from *Super Sentai* became Rita Repulsa in *Power Rangers*. Despite initial misgivings and fears of potential legal dispute, Saban Entertainment was happily surprised to see the show achieve overnight success.

However, most pop culture experts and purists do not view *Power Rangers* favorably despite its popularity in the Western World, and *Super Sentai*, in comparison wins hand over in terms of characterizations of hero and villains, costumes, the background story, and plot lines of each episode.

Speed Racer

This anime series was one of the first exported to the US from Japan. The starting catchphrase of the anime series '*Here he comes, here comes Speed Racer. He's a demon on wheels*' is folklore amongst Speed Racer fans. The original Japanese TV show is called 'Mach GoGoGo,' which was again based on a print-based anime series which appeared in Shueisha's Shonen Book in 1958.

The series in print form was published as a tankobon book later on by Sun Wide Comics. Tankobon, which is Japanese for standalone or independent, is a term meaning a book that is complete in itself without being a part of a bigger corpus or series. Tankobon is a term used typically to refer to manga comic books, which came in complete individual volumes.

Selected sections of the original comic book were published in English by NOW Comics. These comics were titled *Speed Racer Classics*. Sometime later, Wildstorm Productions, a subsidiary of DC Comics, released selected chapters titled *Speed Racer: The Original Manga*.

The TV show, *Mach GoGoGo* produced by Tatsunoko Production Company (an animation company in Japan), was aired from April 1967 to March 1968 on Fuji TV. This TV show depicted amazing car stunts using advanced technology making it one of the most loved shows of all times. The characters in the original show were simple Japanese citizens, and this was one of the primary reasons for its success there.

The protagonist of the show, Go wore ankle-length pants and his car was called Ma-ha Go, or Mach Five. This car was enabled with superior technology and could perform multiple (and almost impossible) stunts such as jumping through the air, developing super-grip wheels on command, slashing and cutting through obstacles with its rotary blade, and more.

Mach GoGoGo represents the name of the protagonist, the name of his car, and an exclamatory aspect. 'Go' in Japanese is used as an exclamatory term. Mach GoGoGo became an instant hit for multiple reasons including simple easy-to-follow plots, lovable characters, and the wonderful tricks that the car was able to perform.

Interestingly, the producer and writer (Tatsuo Yoshida) and director (Tsuyoshi Sasakawa), were not car enthusiasts, and in fact, did not even possess driving licenses!

The fact that they could craft wonderful, engaging stories was sufficient enough to make hit TV animation shows. The protagonist faced numerous exciting challenges from evil-mongers, and this set up was ideal to create stories of revenge, competition, valor, and honor. Some of the stories spanned more than one episode though typically, one episode had one story.

The Japanese creators got their idea for the story of *Mach GoGoGo* from an earlier automobile racing comic stories called *Pilot Ace*. The director, Yoshida, said that his idea for racers and racing cars came from popular America movies such as *Goldfinger* and *Viva Las Vegas* playing in Japan at that time. Yoshida combined the designs from the images of Elvis Presley's race car and Bond's gadget-full Aston Martin to create Mach 5.

Go's rival is a robotic, remote-controlled car that causes plenty of accidents. Go races against this rival car and gains a reputation as a hero who can wreak havoc on dangerous nemeses out to cause harm to the public. Go's power to fight these rivals was so good that he could deal even with those villains that the police couldn't handle. Then, Go's missions went beyond Japan and treaded onto international territories as he globe-trotted all over the world fighting villains and winning races.

Another well-loved feature of this *Mach GoGoGo* was the humor in it. Except for Go (his full name was Go Mifune; in honor of the Japanese film star) who is cool, calm, and collected, all the other characters are depicted as being very human with both strengths and weaknesses. Trixie, Go's girlfriend, is quite a complaining character, and yet can parachute out from a burning plane. Go's father, the creator of Mach 5, is depicted as a brilliant but goofy engineer.

73

Go's little brother, Spritle Racer, is another interesting character in the TV show. Armed in a candy-striped bodysuit and accompanied by his pet monkey called Chim-Chim, he can solve crimes faster than the grownups. Then there was Go's mysterious rival (you'll learn he was Go's older brother), Racer X, whose full name was Rex Racer.

The characterizations in *Mach GoGoGo* are typical of Japanese anime shows. The protagonist is usually a rebellious young boy seeking adventure, a feminine but vociferous and sassy girlfriend, wise but slightly goofy parents, and plenty of cute extra characters make Japanese TV shows (*Mach GoGoGo* was one of the very first) extremely lovable and exportable. All these features clearly distinguish Western TV shows from the Japanese ones, and it looked like the Western world embraced what came from the east.

The first series ran for 52 episodes and was aired on prime time, Sunday evening 7 pm which is when most Japanese families including the kids watched TV together.

In the fall of 1967, *Mach GoGoGo* TV show was released as *Speed Racer* in the US. The rights for the English remake of *Mach GoGoGo* TV show were bought by the American syndicate, Trans-Lux, during the same time. By the way, *Speed Racer* is a translation of the protagonist's name.

For US consumption, Peter Fernandez edited and dubbed the original Japanese episodes using his own voice for many characters, especially Speed Racer and Racer X. Syncing Japanese lip movements to English was challenging, as was writing English scripts for the unfamiliar storylines steeped in Japanese lifestyle and tradition. However, the dubbed versions allowed for multiple parodies driven by the amazingly fast Japanese diction. Very few cartoon TV shows of that era gained as much popularity and sustaining powers as *Speed Racer*.

In the 1990s, the broadcasting rights were bought by other TV channels including MTV and Cartoon Network. Unlike the original *Mach GoGoGo*, the *Speed Racer* series in the 1990s was broadcast at odd hours such as late nights or early mornings. Despite the odd hours, *Speed Racer* gained in popularity, especially among the teens reflecting the influence that Japanese manga had over the western world. Here are some reasons for Speed Racer's popularity in the western world:

- The family structure depicted endeared everyone to the *Speed Racer* TV show.
- Car racing was immensely popular with both adults and children.

- Mach 5 and its amazing ability to perform superhuman tricks.
- There was a highly engaging element in the Speed Racer show and its characters that seemed to be missing in other TV shows of that time.
- Speed Racer-inspired toys and collectibles sustained the interest of children.
- The westernization of the plots and characters gave the show an American appeal.

Moreover, the concept of story-telling in the Americanized version appealed to adults and children, alike. The show had drama, emotion, tension, advanced technology, and everything else to make a complete blockbuster. There was that child dreaming of becoming a big racer right through the day in school (the purist American might have asked, 'when will this child study?'). However, the Japanese mother encouraged her son to dream big and follow his dreams.

The story of the dead brother (who was none other than Racer X) created a great build-up. And above all, the honest and blunt simplicity of the plot and characters seemed to have appealed to the western world.

The *Speed Racer* TV show endeared itself to the US audience so much that Hollywood was ready to make a full-length feature film, which was released in 2008. The *Speed Racer* movie is proof of the never-ending popularity of Japanese pop culture. All its comics' chapters were published in the US by Digital Manga Publishing in 2008 and released as a box set to commemorate Mach GoGoGo's 40th anniversary. The western world is willing and happy to take everything that the island nation is offering and adapting it to Western sensibilities and creating blockbusters of them.

Speed Racer left its influence in other aspects of American life as well. Characters from this show featured in commercials for Geico auto insurance and Volkswagen cars, a multitude of merchandise including toys, action figures, and more. An industrial punk-rock band called themselves Racer X after the Speed Racer character. *Speed Racer* was not limited to a mere TV show or comic book. It consumed America in its Japanese pop culture movement.

Ironically, *Mach GoGoGo* was not as popular in Japan as *Speed Racer* was in the US, baffling many a Japanese anime fan. One of the reasons attributed to the differed response is the timing of the release. When *Speed Racer* was released in the US, the country was already past the happy and prosperous days of post-WWII.

The Vietnam era was taking place, the concept of family was falling apart, and there was a lot of unhappiness around.

People were coming out on the streets and protesting against their own government. *Speed Racer* came like a whiff of fresh air for the Americans reminding them of the lost good old days.

The 1967's *Speed Racer* series was one of the earliest Japanese TV shows to enter the US. And that was only the beginning as many more followed even as Japan continued to borrow ideas from the US. This back-and-forth pop culture between the US and Japan will not end any time in the near future.

Chapter 3: Anime

Understanding Anime and Manga

Japanese anime, many of which have their origins in manga comics, share similar characteristics with cartoons from the rest of the world. Elements of adventure, drama, suspense, comedy, horror, mystery, and love and romance are in anime and manga.

And yet, these Japanese comic genres offer more than just the joy and happiness of watching a cartoon. There are many sub-genres within the manga/anime genre that people outside Japan and the manga world may not know about. These sub-genres target specific audiences and demographics, and everyone in this targeted space, including grownups, watch the anime series drawn from that particular sub-genre of manga books.

Shounen – Shounen, also spelled as shonen, is the most popular sub-genre of anime targeting young male teenagers, and are commonly called boys' comics. The main protagonist of shounen works is a young boy who starts off on exciting adventures in which he will definitely meet extremely feminine and beautiful girls, and of course, numerous evil characters whom he will have to battle and win. The art style of shounen character is angular which is in line with the demography. Popular shounen anime series included *Dragon Ball Z* and *Naruto*.

Shoujo – Shoujo is the female counterpart of shounen targeting young female teenagers. Referred to as girls' comics, the protagonist is a young girl who dreams of idealized romance and faces issues on the path of achieving true love. The characters and the plots are softer than the ones depicted in shounen manga.

Also, the girl protagonists are cute and distinguished rather than being portrayed in an overly sexy manner. The boys in shoujo also tend to be softer, winsomely handsome, and more sensitive to women needs than the protagonists of shounen. The lines in the art style are more rounded than angular to reflect the softness of the characters.

Shoujo Beat is an anthology of shoujo shows, and some popular series included here are *Fushigi Yuugi* and *Fruits Basket*.

Seinen – Typically, these anime series represent grownup shounen characters. Targeted at adult males, seinen anime series can be differentiated from the shounen series based on the content, which will include a lot of adult scenarios that are clearly not suitable for kids. Some popular ones include *Girlfriend*, with a lot of sexual content and *Addicted to Curry*. You can differentiate the characters from other manga sub-genres through the shadows under girls' breasts and undistinguished and ordinary-looking boys and men.

Josei – This sub-genre represents grownup shoujo. Made for women, the series made under this format typically follow the life of the female protagonist. Combining routine life with romance, the plots in josei formats are realistic and relatable. Popular ones include *Honey and Clover* (a rom-com) and *Love Vibes*, a series that follows the love life of two young women.

Kodomomuke – Commonly referred to simply as 'kodomo,' this anime sub-genre targets only children. The stories teach morals and all content is suitable for children in this format. Classic examples include *Astro Boy* and *Hamtaro*. Differentiating this format from others is easy thanks to the extreme levels of cuteness depicted in them, and the inclusion

81

of some animal characters. There will be no adult weird undertones.

We cannot discuss anime without first learning about the 'Godfather of Anime.' So, let's get right in.

Osamu Tezuka – An Introduction

Tezuka Osamu Manga Museum in Takarazuka, Japan.

Anime and manga are the deadliest forms of Japanese pop culture to have been exported out of the island nation, and both these forms would not have been possible if it werent' for one man who took the anime-manga world by storm, Osamu Tezuka. Epithets such as 'Godfather of Anime' and 'Father of Manga' adorn his name. Americans call him 'Walt Disney of Japan.'

Osamu Tezuka revolutionized Japan's global perspective in the post-WWII scenario as it undertook major steps to transition from its military power to the power of technology and pop culture. With over 700 manga titles to his credit spanning over 40 years, Tezuka's artistic ingenuity is no doubt among the best of artists of the world. He is one of the most prolific artists of all times, and definitely the best Japanese manga creator in history.

While his artistic powers play an important role in making Japanese pop culture the most popular one in the world, his influence includes other aspects too. He played an undeniable role in creating and sustaining an industry centered on Japanese manga and anime. He developed manga and comic characters and stories into TV series, and vice versa, and exported them to the entire world, in general, and the western world, in particular.

Early Life of Osamu Tezuka

Born into a family of military, lawyers, and doctors in 1928, Osamu Tezuka was the eldest of three siblings. His passion for manga could have come from his father who was an engineer but was fascinated by manga. Tezuka's home had a big collection of manga; his father saw to it. Moreover, his father was the one who introduced his son to two of his biggest influencers in the future; Walt Disney (who needs no introduction) and Max Fleischer (the creator of *Koko the Clown*, *Betty Boop*, *Superman*, and *Popeye* cartoons).

The exposure to manga and comics at an early age facilitated the creative spirit in Tezuka's mind. He devoured comic books and is known to have watched the blockbuster *Bambi* (the 1942 Walt Disney animated classic) nearly 80 times!

His mother played a big role in influencing his future works. Growing up in Takarazuka City, his mother would take him to the Takarazuka Theater (the members and artists were all women) to see performances. Tezuka based many of the costume designs of his manga characters from what he saw and remembered from his exposure to the works of the Takarazuka Theater.

He started drawing his own manga characters during his elementary school years. His parents were very supportive of his desires and he never felt the dearth of art materials. Then, tragedy struck. He got an infection during his teenage years, and because of which, he nearly lost both his arms. After this incident, Tezuka wanted to become a doctor to help other people just as his doctors helped him through his difficulties. Right through his medical school, he kept his love for manga alive.

While still in medical school, Tezuka sold his first manga to a children's newspaper in Osaka. A simple four-paneled series titled *Diary of Ma-Chan*, this series was his first step into fame. Next, he sold the *New Treasure Island*, which was his first adaptation of a western comic. Most of his early works were influenced by western works considering his access to Disney comics. However, he added his own twist and a unique spin to each of his western adaptations.

When the *New Treasure Island* also met with success, he became a national figure which was a turning point in his career. Enthused by his early success, he sought advice from his mother, should become a full-time mangaka or should he simply take the safe route and become a doctor like so many of family members? Remember that the mangaka profession during his time was nothing like what it is today. In fact, he is responsible for giving credence and commercial success to his art. Before that, being a mangaka meant not earning enough money.

His mother responded like this, "Take up the profession that you love doing." Taking her advice to heart, he focused on and devoted a lot of his time and energies to manga. However, he did not quit medical school. He completed his studies and graduated. He used a lot of his medical education to bring credibility to his manga works.

Astro Boy

In this chapter, we look at one anime series of Osama Tezuka that revolutionized Japanese pop culture which took deep roots in the western world, Astro Boy.

Astro Boy received phenomenal success both in Japan and the rest of the world, especially in the US.

Published between 1952 and 1968 as a manga series, *Astro Boy* needs no introduction in his country of origin where he is called Atom and has become a household name. The protagonist in this futuristic anime is an atomic-powered robot who was created to substitute Dr. Tenma's dead son. When he loses his son, Dr. Tenma is devastated and crippled.

With the hope of filling the void left by his beloved son's death, he creates a robot which he names Tobio. Unfortunately, he believes that the robot is flawed and imperfect. Angry at his work, he discards Tobio. Another professor finds the discarded robot in the rubbish heap and revives him as Atom or the Astro Boy. The wonder robot is given the task of saving Japan and the world from all kinds of threat that could damage humanity while being a role model for all other robots.

Atom is a kind and compassionate robot who has a human heart and is ready to fight for mankind. The timing of the release of Astro Boy is also very important. Japan was struggling from the ravages of WWII and was desperate for peace. The Japanese people were able to relate to the endearing character of Astro Boy who was striving for the same kind of peace that the Japanese people were looking for. Astro Boy became a spokesman for the peace-seeking citizens of the island nation.

Moreover, as the years progressed, *Astro Boy* became a symbol of Japan as it worked its way back to the top of the world with its powers of technology and pop culture. *Astro Boy* became an icon of self-empowerment urging the Japanese people to work and become a role model for the whole world just like how he was a role model for all the robots.

Astro Boy became the first manga to be adapted for animation, and his popularity soared so high that he was no more restricted to his country of birth but a global phenomenon. In the 1960s, *Astro Boy* moved into the anime world and has many 'firsts' to his credit. Let us look at some of them:

He was the first anime to be adapted from an original manga book – Astro Boy's entry into the films and television happened with a live-action movie that released in 1959 when tokusatsu (live-action series with elaborate special effects and grand costumes) was slowly losing its ground.

However, not satisfied with the live-action format, Tezuka founded Mushi Productions, an animation studio, to realize his dream of creating anime with his favorite manga character, Astro Boy. Therefore, the *Astro Boy* anime is the first one to have been originated from a manga character.

The visuals in* Astro Boy *anime still inspires and influences new anime series – At the beginning of its anime journey, Japan looked to China and the US for inspiration regarding settings, immersive animations, and deep characterizations. Tezuka reversed inspired-inspiring roles for Japan with the *Astro Boy* anime series.

He broke down the process of anime creation down to its bare layers and created a unique technique that aligned with and reflected his manga drawings and panels. Using limited animation, and focusing more on the content and story-telling process, Tezuka was able to keep costs down as well as create more heart-touching tales than what his US and the China counterparts were doing at that time.

Some features used in the Astro Boy anime series for the first time that are still in use today include:

- Recycling of animation cels
- Panning the camera across stationary cels to create a sense of movement
- Quick cuts between shots

- Rapidly moving mouth flaps which required dubbing artists to give a voice over instead of using the time-consuming process of creating anime to sync with the voice work

At this point, it makes sense to see what Hollywood elements Tezuka used in the creating of Astro Boy anime series. The adorable features and the wide eyes of Astro Boy are reflective of the cute animated figures of the Disney World. The spikes in his hair look very similar to Mickey Mouse's ears. Tezuka did not adopt these elements unwittingly. He always acknowledged the influence of Disney on his works and creative thinking process.

Astro Boy was the first robot to appear in an anime series – Today, you cannot think of an anime series without an important robot character. Robots that work together in Voltron or human-controlled gigantic robots in the Gundam franchise are all ubiquitous characters in anime. Robots and anime gel with each other as delectably as peanut butter and chocolate.

Astro Boy took a leadership role in this aspect. He was the first robot in an anime series, and others followed suit. Tezuka always intended to change the human perception about robots. Most humans treated robots like property despite the depiction of a bright and amazing future for the machines.

Even in the anime series, Astro Boy was artificially made and traded like a toy slave. Tezuka likened this kind of discriminate human behavior to robots as being reflective of their discriminatory attitude towards any disenfranchised or a minority group. Anti-robot feelings can easily be interpreted as a racist attitude. The *Astro Boy* series shed light on these discriminatory inclinations of human beings.

***Astro Boy was the first 'reluctant hero' in anime* –** Today, every superhero asks questions such as:

- Why me?
- Why should I be the one to do all the dirty work?
- Why should I be the one who should always be fighting?
- Why can't I have the life I want?

As the character of Astro Boy progresses, these and more such questions keep popping up in the episodes. His reluctance and misgivings about his superpowers and his ability to do a lot of good are now part of nearly every superhero. Nearly all anime heroes would rather be ordinary people instead of doing the heroic tasks they are destined to do. And all this is thanks to Astro Boy and Tezuka's intention to give his protagonist great depth of character.

Astro Boy *targeted adults too* – Initially, the audience of *Astro Boy* were young children. However, dark shades emerged as his character progressed through the episodes because Tezuka intended to expand the audience base of anime. He wanted it to be enjoyed by kids as well as adults.

For example, although Astro Boy was saving the day by eliminating the bad guys, the later episodes showed that bad and violent things can happen even to good people. This was not easily accepted by the US audience. In fact, during the initial stages of these changing dynamics, Tezuka received little notes from his US distributors that the content was not really suited for the US audience. Moreover, the distributors aired only 100 of the 200 episodes in the US because they were unsure of the audience reaction to the dark aspects depicted in 'children's fare.'

Tezuka was the first animator who had the nerve and gall to take anime from the children's genre to the adult genre. Of course, it took a lot more time for the US audience to understand and accept this transition.

Astro Boy *was the first anime series to make the American crossover* – Driven by a lot of factors including the increasing interest in the science fiction and the impetus given to space exploration during that time, Astro Boy quickly fit into the popularity charts of the American people. Astro Boy with his ability to fly, rescue people, and have exciting adventures is easily relatable to everyone irrespective of culture and geography.

Other anime classics to cross over to the US from Japan are:

- *Jungle Emperor* – as *Kimba the White Lion* (more about this later in this chapter)
- *Tetsujin 28* – as *Gigantor*
- *Mach GoGoGo* – as *Speed Racer*

Therefore, Astro Boy sparked and kindled American fascination for anime, and it continues to the modern times.

Buddha

Taking the story of Prince Siddhartha who becomes the Buddha, Tezuka created a brilliant manga series that both children and adults enjoy. The series follows the story of the spoiled Prince Siddhartha who had a luxurious childhood and youth that left nothing to the imagination. His father kept him safe from the outside brutal world, and he knew nothing except the rich palace, and pleasure and fun.

Then, one day, his curiosity overtook the desire for riches and wealth, and he leaves behind all his wealth to go in search of spiritual enlightenment. With incredible visuals, Tezuka created an immersive experience for the audience allowing them to plunge into Buddhist scriptures and culture, traveling with the prince-turned-monk through his journeys spreading his knowledge and warning people about the pains of excessive desire.

The narrative is humorous and thought-provoking simultaneously. *Buddha* is one of the last manga epics created by Tezuka, published in Japan between 1972 and 1983, and an anime full-length feature film was released in 2011 that was extremely well-received. Tezuka's popularity in the western is primarily attributed to the *Astro Boy* and *Buddha* series.

Kimba the White Lion

Titled *Jungle Taitei* in Japan, this manga series was published between 1950 and 1954, achieving immense popularity in Japan. Fuji Television aired the anime series from 1965 to 1967 was the first color anime TV series in Japan. The storyline goes as follows:

Set in the jungles of Africa, Panja, the Emperor of the Jungle, was a just and loved king. However, he is killed by a hunter, and his wife is captured. On the way to the zoo, she delivers a baby lion cub named Leo. She advises her son to escape from the ship which is carrying them to the zoo, return to Africa, and take his father's place as the king.

A sudden storm topples the ship, and the mother-son duo fight for their survival in the raging storm. The mother dies, and Leo finds himself washed ashore on a beach of a port town on the Arabian Peninsula. From here, the adventures of Leo begin. The story of Leo is reflective of the condition of Japan at the time it was written. Japan was defeated in WWII and needed to find the strength and power to get back its international stature.

The story of Leo was inspirational to the Japanese as they realized, like Leo did in the anime series, that they need to learn the new ways of the new world and create a niche for themselves. Without any parental guidance and help, Leo learns to become responsible, fighting against adversities at every step of his life to get back his father's kingdom. The anime series served as a metaphor for the struggle and growth of Japan as it found its path back to the pinnacle of glory. Leo's story of self-discovery is emotionally riveting and timeless in character.

The Controversy Surrounding *Kimba the White Lion* and Simba of *The Lion King*

Everyone knows the cuteness and lovability of Simba of *The Lion King*, a movie released in the mid-1990s. Simba became a symbol of the quintessential lovable lion that adults and children swooned over for years. A huge success the world over, Disney leaders proclaimed it was the first cartoon feature movie that was original and not remade from fairy tale classics such as *The Beauty and the Beast* or *The Little Mermaid*.

However, many people were not impressed with this claim of originality. People expressed shock by the many similarities that *The Lion King* shared with *Kimba the White Lion* anime series of the 1960s. The filmmakers at Disney quickly defended themselves saying that they were not influenced by Kimba in any way.

The company declared that the people involved with the making of Simba were not aware of the existence of Kimba. The co-director said that he had no knowledge about the older anime character, and the first time he heard about it was on a trip to Japan to promote *The Lion King*.

However, opponents declared this defense as rubbish because one of the co-directors worked as an animator in Japan during the 1980s when Tezuka was at his peak and when the anime series *Jungle Emperor* was widely viewed on Japanese TV. Animators across the world protested and said that Kimba and Tezuka must have been acknowledged in the Disney movie. The Disney filmmakers remained silent.

Expert animators argued the glaring similarities between the two including the appearance of different characters such as the wise baboon, hyenas, a love-interest in the form of a lioness, and a villain lion too, all of which appear in both Kimba and Simba. Some people involved in the filmmaking process did come out and say that Kimba and Tezuka were discussed.

The animators at Tezuka's Production Company, however, agreed that it is possible that similarities like the ones mentioned by experts can happen if animals are used as characters in cartoons. In fact, many people from the Japanese production house said that Tezuka would have been very pleased if Disney was inspired by his work. And, the controversy came a full circle with both Simba and Kimba achieving immense popularity among anime and cartoon lovers despite the similarities and differences. After all, Tezuka did not bother to hide his own fascination and love for Walt Disney and his works.

Death of Osamu Tezuka and After

Osama Tezuka was an extremely hardworking and committed individual and took the role of an animator very seriously. Stanley Kubrick was so impressed with his work that he wanted Tezuka as an art designer for his magnum opus, *2001: A Space Odyssey*. Tezuka, unfortunately, couldn't take up the offer because he was already very busy in Japan.

Stomach cancer killed this genius mangaka in 1989, but he left a legacy that is timeless. He made mangaka a highly rewarding and respectable profession that the modern youth all across the world want to take up as a career. A workaholic right up to his end, his famous last words were reportedly, "I beg you. Please let me work." His long legacy includes numerous remakes of his works, a big museum, and the influence of his technique even today.

Future generations of Japanese artists including Akira Toriyama and Hayao Miyazaki have named Tezuka and his works as their biggest influences. His fans gave Tezuka a fitting biography. The *Osamu Tezuka Story* was published as a serialized manga series shortly after his death in 1989. In 1992, the final version in a complete book form was published.

The journey of this amazingly large manga book (928 pages in total!) took more than 14 years to reach US shores. Like all manga stories, this non-fiction book on the 'Godfather of Anime and Manga' is read in the legacy of manga from right to left and back to front, and not in the traditional left to right and front to back.

This book was written, designed, and drawn by Toshio Ban, a manga artist (mangaka in Japanese) who worked under the legend for more than 15 years. Ban not only had the responsibility of telling an honest story of his friend and colleague but also had to capture the core essence of Tezuka's distinctive drawing and designing style, which was the ultimate homage he paid to his mentor, colleague, and friend.

Sazae-San

If Tezuka was the Godfather of Manga, there was someone, and a woman at that, who was the Godmother of Japanese Manga too, though she is referred to as the Grandmother of Manga. She is Machiko Hasegawa, and her highly influential work, the *Wonderful World of Sazae-San* created a significant impact on the manga world.

Many Western fans of comics and manga may not be aware of the great Sazae-San character and her creator. *The Wonderful World of Sazae-San* follows the story of a little girl of the same name and her family. The comic depicts the problems she and her family faces as they cope with daily life struggles in the aftermath of WWII.

Hasegawa's 4-panel manga was first published in 1946 and ran every day until 1974. The anime started in 1969 and is still being aired; a Guinness World Record for the world's longest-running anime series. The collected volume of the manga series sold over 62 million copies, and there are numerous live-action movies made on Sazae-San.

Machiko Hasegawa, the genius creator of Sazae-San, was born in Kyushu in 1920. She was the second of three siblings who grew up in Kyushu until her father died when she was 14 years old. Then, the family moved to Tokyo, and she completed her graduation from an all-girls school here.

She started drawing cartoons even as a teenager, and at 16, she apprenticed under Suiho Tagawa, a famous mangaka of that time. Her first manga series *Badger Mask* or *Tanuki no Omen* in Japanese was published in 1938 in a magazine called *Shojo Club*. During WWII, Hasegawa and her family went to live in a seaside town of Fukuoka prefecture where Hasegawa came up with the idea of Sazae-San.

Inspired by the sea, she created the delightful story of Sazae-San and her family. Sazae is a word for shellfish, too. Her younger sister was her sounding board as Hasegawa made notes of her ideas even as she worked in her vegetable garden. *Sazae-San* was first published in April 1946. At the end of 1946, Hasegawa moved back to Tokyo with her family.

With the help of her sisters, Hasegawa established a company that began to publish *Sazae-San* volumes. In December 1949, *Asahi Shimbun*, a reputed newspaper, published the series in their evening edition making Hasegawa the first successful woman mangaka in Japan.

The uniqueness of Sazae-San is that it is unlike all other manga works of that time. There is no cuteness factor, there are no big beautiful eyes or other such lovable manga features. And yet, the character captures your heart and mind as she addressed women issues including the compelling social need to appear 'ladylike.'

You will find Sazae-San walking into a formal introduction scene late and her mouth filled with food. These scenes that are in complete contrast to what is expected from well-behaved Japanese ladies created a feminism flutter across the country much before the concept of feminism took the western world by storm. This anti-ladylike stance and behavior can be seen through the entire manga series.

Despite Sazae-San's rebellious and unladylike attitude, her family is very supportive of her. There are family fights and silly pranks all around. Moreover, this manga strip does not focus solely on Sazae-San. There are plenty of other family depictions which show a variety of characters including parents, kids, wives, husbands, and the elderly.

Despite the obvious gender issues discussed in some of the strips, there are many more that discuss other mundane topics of daily life including poop! However, Hasegawa never missed an opportunity to address gender equality issues and the changing dynamics of Japanese society affected by the WWII defeat. Her comic strips kept pace with the changing times, and for a series that was published for nearly three decades, this aspect is quite obvious to the discerning reader.

For example, Sazae-San wears knee-length skirts in the manga strips published during the 1040s and 1950s. In the 1960s and 70s, Sazae-San has changed to pants and miniskirts. During the 1960s, there was an increased movement of feminism in Japan, and Sazae-San joins a women's group to reflect the changing dynamics in society.

Hasegawa, through Sazae-San, allows you to see into the world of Japanese politics, economics, and society. She gives you a complete tour of Japanese history. The relaxing and wholesome viewing experience that this anime series offers is an endearing factor for its unprecedented longevity.

Although the last *Sazae-San* manga was printed on February 21, 1974, Hasegawa and her intrepid heroine have not lost their sheen or charm. The *Sazae-San* anime series' popularity rate is an indication of Japanese stock market performance. A story (believable or not is up to you) goes like this; if the stock market is on a downward slide, the Japanese people sit at home and watch the *Sazae-San* anime, increasing its TRP ratings, and when the stock market is on a roll, then the TRP rating of *Sazae-San* takes a hit!

While Tezuka deserves every bit of credit and more for his hard work in taking manga to the rest of the world, it would be unfair to leave out Hasegawa from the list of Japanese manga all-time achievers. So, you see the history of Japanese anime is old and rich and is an aspect of Japan life that has entered multiple homes across the world crossing geographical and cultural boundaries.

Gundam

Also referred to as *Gundam Series*, this sci-fi media franchise featuring giant robots called *Gundam*. It started in April 1979 as an anime TV series which became so popular that there was a spawning into other media forms including merchandise, manga, video games, and novels.

Written and illustrated by animator Yoshiyuki Tomino along with a team of creators (the members kept changing) from Sunrise (the production company) that were collectively referred to as Hajime Yatate, *Gundam Series* was targeted primarily for young boys.

Audience for Anime

Anyone can watch anime series and enjoy them. Although the target audience might appear to be only kids and teenagers, you would be surprised how many more people watch these exciting series. Right from the early days of *Astro Boy* and *Speed Racer* to the 90s anime boom with *Pokemon*, *Dragon Ball Z*, and *Sailor Moon*, the quirky characters, great stories, and creative and imaginative worlds, anime's impact on the western world is limitless.

While some believe there is excessive violence and sex in anime, many people across all ages enjoy watching them. Here are some excellent reasons for their success in the western world, especially the US.

The anime series is almost endless – Look at any of the cartoon series from the west, and one of the most disappointing aspects is that they end quickly, and many times are even discontinued. In contrast, Japanese anime series like *Pokemon* and *One Piece* have been going on for years now. Many of the series run for at least 100 episodes, and of course, you know the story of Sazae-San that has been running from 1969, and there doesn't seem to be a finish line yet.

Anime fans do not get the rug pulled out from under their feet suddenly and without warning, which is the case for many western cartoon series.

The background and animation effects are excellent – Nearly all anime series depict visuals that are both stunning and immersive. Studio Ghibli (founded by Hayao Miyazaki) films such as *Princess Mononoke* and *Spirited Away* are classic examples of stunning visuals in the anime format. *Spirited Away* took the western world by storm and people of all ages came away with the effects of the movie running in their minds after it finished.

In fact, the artistic aspect of anime is a separate subject by itself, and some museum's exhibit these anime objects and visuals exclusively for visitors to feast their eyes on. The anime artists creating the visuals are all highly respected and well-paid members of the franchises and are regarded as demigods in their respective domains. This divinity attributed to their work is evident in the anime these amazing artists produce.

There are a lot of adult-genre elements in anime – For example, death is never discussed in any western cartoons. There could be a few deaths such as the death of Simba's father in *The Lion King* or Bambi's mother in *Bambi*. However, the main protagonist will never die. Supporting roles might die;

but the main characters are immortal. Everything is depicted as black and white in western cartoons; heroes and their friends can never do anything wrong or unlawful whereas the villains and the bad men do only wrong, and will never do any good.

In anime, all these are off the radar. There is so much death and destruction depicted, that entire generations of characters can all be massacred together in one episode (for example, the original *Transformer* series that came in the 1980s). Of course, new ones are created and take their place in the next anime. But, even the main protagonists die.

In *Sailor Moon*, characters keep popping off, and their deaths become a turning point in the series resulting in new sets and new plots. No one is safe from death and destruction in anime series making them a highly rewarding experience for adult viewers who can easily relate to such imperfections in life. Of course, there are exceptions even in the anime world. For example, Doraemon and Pikachu are eternal characters, and therefore, kids are also happy with anime!

In addition to death, the story-telling narrative of many anime series makes adult ponder on the philosophies and drives you to question your self-belief and view everything around you in a new light. And, there are anime series that can squeeze out the emotions in you like how some amazing acting by great actors can. Therefore, anime reaches out to every one of all ages. They are not the prerogative of children alone.

Splendid Music Scores – There are great catchy songs and amazing background scores in many anime series, irrespective of genre. You can turn to *Sailor Moon* and *Pokemon* for catchy tunes while many of Studio Ghibli films have enchanting, haunting music scores. Anime is a great place to make your entry into the world of Asian music. There are anime fans in the western world who are addicted to anime because of the music it provides.

Anime series are made in different sub-genres targeting different sets of people. Therefore, anime covers nearly everyone who enjoys a good, engaging, and entertaining story.

Akira

The cyberpunk anime feature film, *Akira*, was released in Japan on July 15, 1988, much before Marvel made its entry into mainstream cinema. It was released in the US in the following year. This anime showed the western world that cartoons can do more than give you simple, wholesome entertainment. They can solve big humanity problems as well.

Directed by Katsuhiro Otomo, *Akira* is set in the year 2019 and tells the story of Shotaro Kaneda. He is the leader of a biker gang in a dystopian community in Neo-Tokyo, a futuristic metropolis. Shotaro's friend, Tetsuo Shima, acquires amazing telekinetic powers after a freak accident. Rebellions and chaos saturate the film when a huge disaster consumes Neo-Tokyo resulting in World War III. Violent protests lead by marauding biker gangs are repeated scenes in the movie. During one of these protests, Tetsuo meets with an accident in which his bike is completely destroyed. He, however, inexplicably gains amazing telekinetic powers. He uses these powers to discover the threat of an attack from supernatural beings.

As the movie progresses, we learn that the disaster which consumed Neo-Tokyo was caused by Akira, a child with such amazing supernatural abilities that they are beyond human comprehension. The story is an allegory of the atomic bombings on Nagasaki and Hiroshima with Akira representing the atom bombs, and Tetsuo representing the next calamity. *Akira* became a global cult film.

Akira inspired many popular Hollywood movies and shows including:

- Eleven is a kid in the popular Netflix show, *Stranger Things*. Like Akira and Tetsuo, Eleven has amazing supernatural powers. The people behind the making of this Netflix series said that they were highly influenced by the 1988 anime feature film, *Akira*.
- Rian Johnson's movie, *Looper,* was also inspired by *Akira*. In *Looper*, the child character kills his potential assassin using only his mind powers.
- Kanye West's music video, "Stronger", has numerous shot-by-shot retakes from this cult film. He also uses a Japanese artist for his album cover art.
- Supreme, the popular clothing brand, released an apparel line inspired by the artworks in *Akira*.

Akira swept the US coast like a hurricane bringing with it the power and promise of anime to the country. *Akira* made it clear to the American population how cool, popular, and outstanding anime can be. It made the US people sit up and notice that anime is not just for kids but also for adults. The visual effects of *Akira* left them stunned thinking that Japan's movie industry can do even more powerful things than what the highly revered George Lucas' Industrial Light and Magic can create.

Akira made it clear to America, in particular, and the world, in general, that anime is more than cartoons. It can narrate compelling tales using fantastic voice acting and stupendous animation making the outcome even better than the already-popular live-action format.

The anime works of Japan have had a lasting impression in the western world, and as can be seen from the craze for this format of Japanese pop culture, the impact is bound to last for a very long time to come.

Chapter 4: Manga

Manga is the heart of Japanese pop culture. From *Sazae-San* to *Naruto* to *One Piece* to *Doraemon*, manga books have been the central core of Japanese culture. Most of the anime series would not have existed if not for manga books. Anime producers draw from the manga well because they were not willing to risk their resources on stories and characters that haven't proven their popularity.

The Origin of Manga

Manga is believed to have its origins in a series of 12th and 13th-century drawings called Choju-giga or the Scrolls of Frolicking Animals. Several artists during that time were drawing these pictures of rabbits, frogs, and other animals, and it is a widely accepted belief that this was the first manga of Japan. The techniques used by the authors to draw these animal characters are used even by the modern-day mangakas.

In the modern times, Isao Shimizu, a researcher and author, defines manga as popular artwork-based story books sold to the masses. Shimizu opines that the first manga work was *Toba Ehon*, a book of drawings accompanied by a story on the lives of ordinary people during the Edo Period (1603-1867). *Toba Ehon* was published and sold in the 18th century by a publisher in Osaka.

The 20th century magazines and newspapers printed comic strips to increase readership. However, the largest contributors to the increase of manga popularity are the monthly and weekly comic magazines that were printed and published in the 1960s. These comic magazines carried about 10-20 series installment per edition. These comic magazines were the platforms for manga artists, and without them, mangakas would not have flourished.

The Connections between Manga and Japanese Mythology

The deeper you read manga books, the more connections you will find between them and Japanese myths and legends. Some of the manga series borrow more than others from ancient Japanese stories. Some of them have a close resemblance to the characters from these age-old legends of the island nation. Here are some examples that clearly connect the two uniquely Japanese elements, manga and Japanese myths:

The Goddess Amatérasu leaving her Retreat.

Amaterasu leaving her Retreat

118

Episode 137 of **Naruto: Shippuden** – In the world of Naruto, Amaterasu is the fire technique that has the power to destroy and annihilate everything it touches. This technique has the power to destroy fire itself. Amaterasu is the sun goddess in Shintoism, the ancient religion of Japan. She was born from the left eye of Izanagi. The firing technique in Naruto also originates from the left eye of the protagonist.

At the end of the same episode, a nine-tailed fox appears. In Shintoism, this creature is considered to be one of the wisest and most powerful beings on earth.

Episode 42 of **Naruto: Shippuden** - Orochimaru is a pale individual who makes an appearance in episode 42. In Japanese folklore, Orochimaru is a character in The Tale of the Gallant Jiraiya in which he was initially a follower of Jiraiya, an omnipotent ninja warrior who held the power of toad magic. During the course of the story, Orochimaru falls under the effects of snake magic, and becomes Jiraiya's arch rival.

In the world of *Naruto*, Orochimaru is one of the main villains and, like his namesake in Japanese folklore, is also feared for snake-inspired powers. Also, Orochimaru uses a technique called Rashomon, which is a famous gate in ancient Kyoto and Nara.

The Popularity of Manga in Japan and the Western World

Manga books sell millions of copies each year in Japan. *One Piece*, *Naruto*, and others speak of readership in millions. Here is a small list of manga sales number in Japan for the period between November 2017 and May 2018:

- *One Piece* –3.1 million copies
- *Attack on Titan* – 2.99 million copies
- *The Seven Deadly Sins* – 2.76 million copies

The above list is only a small illustration of the power of manga books in Japan.

Let us compare these numbers with comic books sold in the US (these are figures for the period January 2017 until November 2017):

- *Marvel Legacy* – 300,000 million copies
- *Dark Nights: Metal No.2* – 270,000 million copies
- *Doomsday Clock No.1* – 240,000 million copies

The sales figures between the US and Japanese markets are not even in the comparable range showing how popular manga books are in Japan. And manga sales in the US continue to rise and experts believe that it is only a matter of time when US comic books will be second to manga books even in the US.

Weekly Shonen Jump

This magazine is a weekly manga anthology under the Jump umbrella of Japanese magazines. It is the longest-selling and the best-selling manga magazines of all times. The first issue of the *Weekly Shonen Jump* was dated August 1, 1968. All the manga series in this weekly magazine target young boys, and therefore, have a lot of action scenes as well as comedy. All the chapters of the various manga series are collected together and published as tankobon volumes once every 2-3 months.

The magazine's circulation was at its peak during the period between the mid-80s and the mid-90s with more than 6.5 million copies sold every week. The numbers as of the beginning of 2017 were about 1.7 million copies per week. An estimated 8 billion manga book copies have been sold by *Weekly Shonen Jump* since its first issue in August 1968. Lasting Manga Works from Osamu Tezuka.

This section deals with some of the most famous works of this anime giant that crossed over to the western world and broke multiple commercial success records.

The Lost World

Titled *Zenseiki* in Japanese, this work was published in Japan in during the late 1940s and early 1950s and came to the US in 2003 under the title, *The Lost World*. *Zenseiki* was the first of Tezuka's series of sci-fi manga books. In this anime series, some scientists discover a rogue planet that is approaching earth. A study team comprising of scientists and other characters find a land inhabited by dinosaurs.

A group of crooks is also kept as prisoners in the spaceship. This study team has to continuously battle the dinosaurs as well as the crooks who snuck into the ship. The anime series is replete with dazzling imaginative drawings and some great plots, too catching the western world in this highly immersive whirlpool of dinosaurs and crooks challenging the good scientists who are out to protect and save the earth.

Metropolis

Titled *Metoroporisu* in the Japanese language, *Metropolis,* a story where robot servants and humans live together, was created in the year 1949 in Japan. The protagonist is a young girl who wants to find her lost parents even though she is unaware that she is a robot-slave and not a human being.

There are, of course, the villains who want to capture this little girl and use her powers for evil purposes. This anime series has been made into a feature-length anime movie as well. The girl is considered to be the precursor to the most famous Tezuka character, Astro Boy.

Next World

Known as *Kurubeki Sekai* in Japanese and published in 1951, this anime, creation of Tezuka has two of the most prominent characters who keep appearing in other anime series as well, Mr. Mustachio and Rock, a boy reporter. The two of them are on a hunt of mutant creatures with harmful intent who have suddenly appeared on earth. Mr. Mustachio and Rock traverse the length and breadth of Earth trying to find and control these mutants.

Princess Knight

Published in Japan between 1953 and 1968, *Ribon no Kishi* (the Japanese title) was one of the few manga series of Tezuka's that was based on a princess. Raised as a boy, but as she grows older, her feminine side yearns to show itself. Replete with romance, royal intrigue, adventure, and magic, this manga series came to the US in 2011 and has caught the imagination of the US kids.

Crime and Punishment

Christened *Tsumi To Batsu* in Japanese, this manga series was published in Japan in 1953, and in the US, in 1990. Tezuka used the plot of Fyodor Dostoevsky's book, *Crime and Punishment* to create this series. The protagonist is Raskolnikov, a poor Russian peasant (yes, the same name of Dostoevsky's protagonist) who murders an old woman because she was a loan shark, and causing a lot of distress to many borrowers who were unable to pay back her loans.

The rest of the series progresses on this premise, and as the reader, you are left guessing whether the endearing protagonist will get away with the crime or will he get caught?

This work of Tezuka focuses on the realities of life and delves into more mature themes that are meant for adults.

Although this manga series is really for hardcore Tezuka fans, its out-of-print status for a long time is driving demand, and scarce secondhand copies are taking on the status of art collector's item. That's how popular and powerful Tezuka's manga series have become, worthy of being in an art collection!

Apollo's Song

Published in 1970 in Japan as *Apollo no Uta*, this story was translated into English in 2007. The hero of the manga series is Shogo who has nothing to be happy about. He was an unintended child who did not know his father as he was born after his mother had a string of affairs. She did not want him, and she beat him often to reflect this attitude. He had an abusive childhood because of which he swore never to be affected by love and lived a hateful violent life.

Seeing his condition, the gods decided to do something about it, and they cursed him to find unconditional love, and then lose it for some reason. Tezuka's powerful story-telling abilities drawn from real-life scenarios tug at your heartstrings. Shogo's struggle to find eternal love and his internal conflicts are what make Shogo a well-loved character with manga readers. His desperation can bring tears to even the hard-hearted reader, and that is the power of Tezuka's illustrations and writing.

Dark theme, indeed, as Tezuka moves deliberately from a children audience to an adult audience!

Dororo

Titled *Dororo* in both Japan and the US, this series was published in 1967-68 in Japan and in 2008 in the US. Replete with action and monsters, this manga series' main protagonist is Hyakkimaru, a wandering warrior. Readers follow his adventures through a combination of samurai drama and manga fantasy stories and backgrounds.

The darker aspects of life are now visible as Tezuka progresses on his manga journey. He started writing for the adult audience too. For example, in *Dororo*, Hyakkimaru is born without many body parts and vital organs, a feature that is definitely not for kids. He is born that way because of his father's duels with many demons. Now, the adventures of

Hyakkimaru include battles with these demons which he must win so that he can regain his body parts and vital organs.

You can notice a shift in Tezuka's approach to writing and creating manga books. His works now include dark aspects of human life, and he is drawing adults into the manga dream world as well.

Black Jack

Published first in 1973, *Black Jack* draws a lot of inspiration from Tezuka's own life. The protagonist, Kuro Hazama, more famously known as Black Jack, is an unlicensed surgeon with amazing and miraculous talent. The character was scarred during his childhood and was saved from near-death by a surgeon.

As a give-back to society, Black Jack also decides to become a surgeon (similar to Tezuka's early life). All the stories follow the good deeds of Black Jack as he goes about treating the poor for free, curing deadly diseases, and teaching villains a lesson. Tezuka uses a lot of his medical school knowledge to add credibility to this surgeon manga series. Even the most outlandish surgeries appear believable in the skilled hands of the doctor turned mangaka Tezuka.

The first anime series was aired in 2003, and other seasons aired after that too. Films and live-action series have also been filmed and aired both in Japan and the US.

Phoenix

Titled *Hi no Tori*, this manga series ran for more than two decades in Japan, from 1967 until 1988. In the US, the *Phoenix* was published between 2003 and 2008. This time-traveling epic is a story of births, deaths, good and evil, and redemption. Considered to be Tezuka's masterpiece, *Phoenix* is the story of a firebrand immortal bird that is a witness for several other beings who die and are reborn repeatedly to achieve redemption.

Artistic innovation, jaw-dropping beauty, and amazing storytelling combine together wonderfully to give readers this astonishing epic in manga form. Again, a series for the adults rather than for the children!

Despite the fairly large number of manga series that are published in the US, there are many, many more that haven't left the shores of Japan. A lot of manga series of Tezuka's are unpublished because there are so many of them, and the entire process of publishing them in the US which includes translating and licensing is a time-consuming and difficult task.

However, thanks to the internet-connected modern world, manga fans are working with various crowd-funding options to print new editions of Tezuka series, all of which still hold the amazing appeal and visceral emotions that existed when they were first created by the 'Godfather of Manga.'

Other Lasting Manga Works

One Piece

One Piece is a manga series created by Eiichiro Oda. The protagonist is Monkey D. Luffy who accidentally eats the devil fruit known as the Gum fruit after which he gains rubber-like quality allowing his body to stretch and expand interminably. This manga was launched in 1996, and since then has gained a global fan base, thanks to the great narrative, humor, and character development.

Luffy becomes the captain of a band of pirates called Straw Hat Pirates. Each devil fruit has different powers, and our hero eats one which gives him rubber-like qualities. Unfortunately, eating a devil fruit makes the eater unable ever to swim. The irony of a pirate captain unable to swim is not lost on the readers.

Luffy's purpose is to find One Piece, the lost treasure of the dead Pirate King Gold Roger. On finding One Piece, Luffy will become the new Pirate King. Every member of the Straw Hat Pirates gang has his own purpose and dream he wants to achieve. As they travel through their sea world, the Straw Hat

Pirates encounter numerous enemies as well as rival pirate gangs who are also after One Piece.

When Oda started writing the stories of *One Piece*, he wanted the tale to end after five years. However, the stories never ended, and new ones continue to be released to this day.

One Piece is considered to be the most successful manga series ever to be created in Japan, achieving popularity worldwide, too, among people of all ages. An anime series was produced and released by Toei Animation in 1999 and has aired more than 700 episodes since then. Also, Toei produced eight special shows for TV and 12 movies based on *One Piece*.

Dragon Ball

Dragon Ball was created by Akira Toriyama originally as a gag manga (humorous manga) that later on evolved into an action-packed martial arts manga. In fact, *Dragon Ball* set new standards for future shonen manga books. *Dragon Ball* was first published in November 1984 in *Shonen Jump Weekly*, the popular weekly manga magazine in Japan.

Every week, a new chapter or episode was published which was approximately 14 pages long. When *Dragon Ball* finished its run in 1995, there were a total of 520 chapters including one side story. The tankobon (the one-volume book containing all the stories of *Dragon Ball*) was published in 2002.

Akira Toriyama's inspiration for *Dragon Ball* was the Chinese novel named *Journey to the West*. Son Goku is the protagonist of the manga, and the storyline follows his journey from childhood to adulthood. The purpose of his life is to collect the seven Dragon Balls. When all of them are collected, these orbs can summon a dragon which could grant wishes.

As he travels all over looking for and collecting the Dragon Balls, Son Goku encounters villains with whom he has to battle as well as friends who help him in his search. Two anime series, *Dragon Ball* and *Dragon Ball Z*, were released by Toei Animation which ran from 1986 to 1996 in Japan.

Dragon Ball is one of the most successful manga franchises of all times, selling over 159 million copies in Japan alone, and over 300 million copies worldwide.

Golgo 13

First published in October 1968, *Golgo 13*'s creator is Takao Saito, and the publication ended in October 2015, one of the longest-running manga series. This manga series follows the story of an assassin for hire and has been made into two live-action movies, an anime film and TV series, and video games too.

Known by his pseudonym, Duke Togo, Golgo 13 is a professional assassin for hire. No one knows his age and birthplace. His complete anonymity in the intelligence world is baffling. He uses a customized M16 rifle for all his assassination jobs. His other aliases include Togo Rodriguez and Tadashi Togo.

With a very quiet personality and minimal conversation, Golgo 13 shows little or no emotion when he is doing his work. He is willing to eliminate any person who threatens to expose him. He will kill anyone for anyone who can pay for his services. His victims range from the simpleton right up to government heads and big political figures.

His assassinations have earned him the wrath of many federal agencies including the CIA, FBI, and the US Army. They are all out to kill him making him very vulnerable. He is always watching out for lurking assassins and killers out to get him even as he completes his own assassination jobs.

Golgo 13 also employs other people to help him with his jobs. These people help him get information about his victims or to customize gadget, vehicles, and weapons for special situations. The phrase Golgo 13 is a reference to the crucifixion of Jesus Christ. Golgo is short for Golgotha where Jesus was crucified, and his logo is a skeleton with a crown of thorns.

In an interview in 2015 after the last episode was printed and published, *Golgo 13*'s creator, Takao Saito made the following points about his favorite character and his own writing journey:

- His coolness and his calculated approach to death endeared him to many adult readers.
- The passion of the readers is what drove him to write 556 episodes; when he started Saito thought that *Golgo 13* did not have a life after 10 episodes.
- *Golgo 13* has murdered and womanized his way into the hearts of millions of fans.
- The character became a trailblazer for graphic novels in Japan.
- He has inspired best-selling business books and countless collectibles.
- He has seen a wide range of reasons to kill; from human trafficking to currency manipulation of the US government to mineral rights negotiation in Africa, and more.
- He is an unsmiling misogynist and yet has captured the hearts of millions of fans in Japan and abroad.
- He can be likened to James Bond but minus softeners in the form of characters like Moneypenny, Q, M, and other fancy gadgets.

- He worked relentlessly as a hitman through the various stages of the changing dynamics of the economic world.
- Duke Togo is the ultimate hoodwinker who fulfilled his contracts meticulously and solved all problems of his clients .
- The enduring and patient nature of Golgo 13 makes him a hardcore and pure Japanese man, and definite samurai.
- His code of conduct is highly impressive; he would never kill without reason. For example, if he found an ant under his foot, he would deftly sidestep and not kill the creature. For Golgo 13, the life of an ant and the life of a human had equal value. He killed only those for whom he received payments.

Kochira Katsushika-Ku Kameari Kōen-Mae Hashutsujo

The first manga series to reach 200 volumes and one of the longest-running of all time, Kochira Katsushika-ku Kameari Kōen-mae Hashutsujo (shortened to Kochikama) is a best-selling gag (comedy) series, unlike most other series which are based on sports, battle, and adventure. It was first published in Japan in 1976 and the last one was published in 2016. The English title is *Kochikame: Tokyo Beat Cops*.

During the entire 40-year run, it did not miss a single issue in the weekly magazine *Shonen Jump* despite its creator Osamu Akimoto being busy with multiple other projects simultaneously. Around 2000 chapters were published, all of which were collected into 200 tankobon volumes. The manga series was also made into an anime series, anime feature films, several stage productions, and live-action movies.

The protagonist name in Kochikama is Kankichi "Ryo-san" Ryotsu, a middle-aged cop who keeps coming up with multiple money-spinning schemes by either creating gadgets or capitalizing on a new fad. With every scheme, he hopes to achieve success; but, things go sour, and he reaches out to Keiichi Nakagawa for help. The humor in the stories comes from a combination of ordinary, everyday characters and completely bizarre and out-of-the-world situations and people. So, you have the extremely wealthy Nakagawa starring alongside Ai Asato, a transgender in many of the stories.

The series takes place in contemporary Japan, and the setting is around a police station, or koban, in downtown Tokyo. The plots are inspired by the current events although the characters in Kochikama never age. The reader can relate to events that took place in the real world from 1976 until 2016 when the manga series ended. Interestingly, the audience for Kochikama ranges from the little children who can laugh at Ryo-San's buffoonery to the adults who can laugh at the mocking satire presented by the stories about the latest fads of the times.

The stories are all innocent, simple, and have no violence at all. Occasionally, risqué topics were discussed; though, it was only to get a laugh or two and never to titillate. The immense popularity of this series is reflected in the fact that huge celebrities such as Tetsuya Komuro (the famous Japanese music producer and musician) made guest appearances in it.

The creator, Osamu Akimoto, said that this manga series was an homage to the working class society in Japan settled in old Tokyo. Many of the stories opened with an illustration of a downtown street scene featuring old wooden buildings and boys playing on the street, a typical scene of old Tokyo.

Doraemon

Talking about Japanese manga without bringing *Doraemon* into the conversation is impossible. *Doraemon* is one of the most beloved and endearing manga series that has captured the hearts of the entire globe, especially the western world. The adorable robotic cat is a huge contributor to its worldwide success.

Doraemon is a cat that travels through time sent to protect and help a sweet and innocent little boy, Nobita Nobi, who is prone to getting into trouble. The episodes follow the story of these two characters as Doraemon employs multiple futuristic gadgets to save Nobita from his troubles. Invariably, with fumbling Doraemon's help, Nobita's problems get worse before getting better enhancing the fun element of the stories.

Illustrated and written by Fujiko F. Fujio, Doraemon was first published in December 1969, and the last episode was published in 1996 and was made into a very popular TV anime series, feature films, video games, and a musical as well. As of 2015, over 100 million copies of *Doraemon* manga series have been sold in over 30 nations. There is a museum in Doraemon's honor which opened in Kawasaki in 2011. Today, Doraemon is easily one of the most recognizable manga characters of all time as he spreads cheer and joy to kids all over the world.

Bleach

Created by Tite Kubo and first published in August 2001, *Bleach* follows the story of Ichigo Kurosaki who gets supernatural powers of a Soul Reaper when he comes across a lady named Rukia Kuchiki from the Soul Society. He gets her powers by accident and has to do her duties until Rukia can get her powers back. He has to defend human beings from evil spirits and also to guide departed souls to the afterlife. The story gets complicated as Ichigo discovers his own mysterious past.

Bleach was published in *Weekly Shonen Jump* as serials from August 2001 until August 2016 and was made into an anime TV series which ran in Japan and the western countries (in the language of the respective country) including France, Spain, Germany, Brazil, and Portugal, in addition to English. The anime series has stories that are not found in the manga books.

Slam Dunk

Even if you don't know anything about basketball, you will love this manga series. Created by Takehiko Inoue and first published in 1990 (the last one was published in 1996), this manga series follows the story of a gang leader named Hanamichi Sakuragi. He meets a girl, Haruko Akagi, in high school who introduces him to Shohoku High School's basketball team. After a series of twists and turns in the story, Sakuragi joins the school squad and learns how friendship and camaraderie can create lifelong allies.

Sakuragi is impetuous and a little immature, and this innocent profile endears him to his girl and fans equally. Made naturally athletic, he wants to impress Haruko and the story's twists and turns come from his attempts to get onto the school basketball team. Kaede Rukawa is a rival in the story which enhances the excitement of episodes. *Slam Dunk* was made into a TV anime series produced by Toei Animation and broadcasted across the globe.

Oishinbo

This manga series is not very well-known outside of Japan. However, in the country of its origin, it is extremely popular and has made it to the top-selling manga series of all times. This foodie manga series follows the story of Shiro Yamaoka, a food journalist. He works with his colleague-turned-wife, Yuko Kurita, and they both create the Ultimate Menu project. The episodes follow and highlight different gourmet dishes.

Written by Akira Hanasaki and Tetsu Kariya, this seinen series is not an action-packed one but has a loyal fan base across the country and was published from 1983 until 2008. The timing was aligned with the gourmet boom in Japan, which contributed to its popularity in the country. Anime and video games were also made.

Detective Conan

The *Detective Conan* manga series follows the story of a high-school detective boy called Jimmy Kudo. IIe is actually a man who gets turned into a high school boy by the Black Organization, a crime syndicate by forcing him to consume a particularly potent poison concocted by one of their members. Taking on the alias of Conan Edogawa, Jimmy Kudo gets back his detecting legacy by solving cases with his high school buddies.

Jimmy lives with his childhood friend, Rachel Moore, and her father, Richard. Richard is a private detective, and Jimmy follows his cases closely. When he is able to solve any case, Jimmy tranquilizes Richard, and using a voice modifier to sound like Richard, he reveals the solution of the case to the police.

During the course of the story, Jimmy meets with Anita Hailey who is also his schoolmate. She reveals her true identity Jimmy; she was the poison maker when she was part of the Black Organization, and by ingesting it, she has also become a little girl. She, however, is no longer affiliated with the crime syndicate and joins Jimmy's detective brigade.

Written by Gosho Aoyama, it was first published in *Weekly Shonen Jump* in January 1994 and continues to be published even today. In English, the series was renamed as *Case Closed* because of some legal implications regarding the name Detective Conan. Anime films, TV series, television specials, and video games were also made.

Naruto

Another extremely popular shonen manga series, *Naruto* was written and illustrated by Masashi Kishimoto and published in the *Weekly Shonen Jump* from 1999 to 2014. *Naruto* comes in two parts, one covering the main protagonist's pre-teens and the second covering his teenage period.

In Japan, *Naruto* was serialized into an anime TV series covering 220 episodes from 2002 to 2007 with the English version airing on Cartoon Network from 2005 to 2009. Then, followed the sequel to *Naruto* called *Naruto: Shippuden* was broadcast in Japan from 2007 to 2017, after completing 500 episodes. The English version of the sequel was aired on Disney XD from 2009 to 2011. *Naruto* was also made into eleven movies and original video adaptations. Additionally, *Naruto* inspired merchandise, video games, novels, and trading cards.

The series follows the story of Naruto Uzumaki, a teenage ninja, who wants to impress his peers. He also desires to become the Hokage, or the leader of his village. The story begins when Nine-Tails, a powerful fox attacks Konoha, a ninja village, whose leader, the Fourth Hokage, was Naruto's father. After a bitter duel, the Fourth Hokage seals Nine-Tails in his son's body after which he loses his life.

Naruto does not know about this incident until he is 12 years old, and the rest of the story follows the hero through various ninja battles even as he attempts to win praises and recognition from his peers (they used to ridicule him because he was the host for Nine-Tails) and dreaming of becoming his village's Hokage.

The world of manga has captured the imagination not only of Japan and its people but the entire world. The beautiful illustrations, amazing stories ranging from comedy to violence to heart-wrenching tales of sorrow have made fans all over the world breaking and crossing cultural and geographical barriers.

Chapter 5:
Trading Ideas between US and Japan

When you start listing the items of Japanese pop culture that have invaded the western world, especially the US, the list is endless. From the earliest *Speed Racer* anime series, the flow has not stopped. Top Hollywood celebrities like M. Night Shyamalan and Leonardo DiCaprio are both connected to anime projects.

Multiple cartoon networks and studios in the US including Spike, IFC, Cartoon Network, and more have popular anime series broadcast regularly on their channels. Walk into any popular bookstore such as Barnes and Noble (closed a few years ago) and you will find shelves and racks filled with manga books.

Anime conversations are not limited to movie celebrities and producers. The average American citizen can have long anime conversations with the most avid manga fan from Japan. There are dedicated J-Pop malls, which have a theater where only Japanese movies are played and other stores that display

Japanese stuff exclusively. Names such as *Pokemon*, *Doraemon*, and others, which were alien-sounding have now become household names.

One of the main reasons for Japanese pop culture to have invaded US markets with such great intensity is the kawaii factor; the ultra-cute Japanese design that permeates anime, manga, and all other Japanese products. Roland Kelts, the author of the book *Japanamerica: How Japanese Pop Culture Has Invaded the U.S.* and Tokyo professor, says that the idea behind kawaii is that when you see it, you not only feel love or find it extremely cute; it is something you would want to protect. Japanese pop culture combines cuteness, playfulness, and coolness.

So, why are Japanese products so popular in the US? Japan was once a mysterious and remote country steeped in incomprehensible Oriental culture. But, today, America is one of the closest allies of Japan. Business ties between the nations are at an all-time high. Why is this happening and why is Japanese pop culture so popular in the US?

Experts believe that one primary reason is that Japanese pop culture has managed to fuse with the US culture and become one with it. Japanese pop culture is not taught in a separate classroom nor is it an exclusive thing. It seems to have merged with American culture. Manga is a classic example of this merger.

The entry and flow of manga into American culture has opened the eyes of the average American to Japan and what it stands for. Look at Pikachu, the cute Pokemon. He is not the average American superhero. He is steeped in Japanese myth and folklore. And yet, he is part of American culture. You will find Pikachu's image alongside that of Superman, Batman, and the Avengers. Pikachu is not exclusive Japanese; he has merged with US cartoons and become of them, despite his distinctive Japanese profile.

America is a multicultural society, which has embraced Japanese food, manga, anime, and other cultural elements with an open heart. Mass media and marketing have helped in the spread of Japanese pop culture across the nation. Then, derivative products are then designed and released as well. These snowball into an avalanche and soon, the same item is available in different forms.

So, manga came first as a comic series. Then, the anime TV series followed. Toys and collectibles based on these manga characters filled the shelves of departmental stores. These multi-pronged activities gathered steam as it rolled into each other catching the attention of the American consumer.

Another reason for the increased popularity of Japanese pop culture is that the Japanese language education is now part of many universities' ecosystems. Universities offer multiple Japan-based educational programs for students undergoing Japanese studies either as a major or minor.

An increase in Japanese language courses so more Americans learn the language, which, in turn, makes understanding Japanese pop culture forms easier than before. The merging with American pop culture is being made seamlessly smooth. Fellowship opportunities and teaching positions are available in many US universities for graduates of Japanese studies.

Japanese Television Trading

Profits for Japanese TV companies increased because of American television bringing in Japanese anime to America. Japanese anime is a niche market in the US today and mainstream anime programs are very successful on multiple US networks such as Sy-Fy, MTV, and Cartoon Network.

Cartoon Network was one of the first American TV companies to embrace anime. They created a new block called Toonami and put all Japanese anime under this program block. Initially, Toonami was dedicated only to American cartoon short films. However, Cartoon Network started mass importing anime in 1999, and anime programs were fit into the Toonami block which ran on all weekdays from 4 pm to 6 pm. Toonami was the only exclusive programming on American TV that focuses on Japanese anime. The ratings of Toonami soared like a behemoth when *Dragon Ball Z* was imported and aired.

The next trading behemoth was Gundam Suits, which resulted in several Gundam shows releasing in the US. Some of these popular Gundam shows include *G-Gundam* and other programs. Of course, the market reached over-saturation with

Gundam even though the anime series is still quite popular among the American boys.

Globalization allows Japanese TV companies to increase profits by allowing their shows to cross over to foreign lands. In the older days of anime transfer, the Japanese shows were only translated into English and aired in the US. But live action shows such as *Super Sentai* went beyond translations and created America-exclusive shows like *Power Rangers* by using only the action parts from the Japanese versions. These adaptations needed American actors to replace the Japanese actors resulting in extra costs which they managed to counter by using the ready action scenes from Japanese shows.

Power Rangers became an overnight success despite these seeming dilutions of artwork and raked in the moolah for both the Japanese and the American companies involved in its making.

Pokémon became another behemoth pop culture element that took American business by storm. Starting off as a video game, soon, *Pokemon* became popular in a wide variety of media platforms including anime, movies, collectibles, merchandising, and more. Everything with Pokémon on it was consumed by the American masses making all the companies involved in it wealthy.

America's Cultural Impact on Japan

Not only has Japanese pop culture invaded the US, the reverse trend is also happening; US pop culture is coming to Japan. American culture in Japan is proliferating in ways beyond the ubiquitous fast-food chains and other pop-culture offerings like rock and pop music.

The Japanese have a big obsession with everything American. This obsession has led to a market that only is great for blockbuster Hollywood movies and popular US beer brands but also a place that can get rarefied versions of American culture such as classic blues and country music.

The Japanese industrialists are looking at taking over American brands and making it better or more suited to Japanese sensibilities. For example, in 2014, Suntory, an Osaka-based well-known whiskey manufacturer acquired Beam Inc., thus becoming owners of international whiskey brands such as Maker's Mark and Jim Beam.

The takeover does not stop with American goods. The Japanese have this innate ability to borrow elements from other cultures and make them better and give them back to the world. We have already seen how huge Japanese directors and filmmakers have been inspired by Hollywood's movies and filmmaking techniques and used them to make Japanese films.

Similarly, they have imitated and made better many foreign elements including cocktails, fashion, food, films, music, cartoons, and more. There are great French chefs and amazing Neapolitan pizzaioli among the Japanese people. They don't just copy but make what they have copied better.

Japan and the US have come together as great business allies after the devastating effects of WWII making the relationship symbiotic as both countries have learned and been influenced by each other for the greater good of both nations.

****

Can you help us?

If you enjoyed this book, then we really appreciate if you can post a short review on Amazon. We read all the reviews and your feedbacks will help us improve our future books.

If you want to leave a private feedback, please email your feedback to: feedback@dingopublishing.com

Thank You..

****

Conclusion

The impact of Japanese pop culture on the western civilization is here to stay. The country's defeat in WWII seemed to have cleared its minds, thoughts, and spirits empowering them to see the true value of Japan across the globe.

The leaders and the people realized that military and economic might is an excellent show-off element. But, capturing the hearts of everyone through their pop culture is even better. Backed by this realization, the Japanese people got down to work and created a popular culture with amazing powers that broke many geographical and cultural boundaries of the world, especially the western world.

The history of Japan is filled with stories, and the legends and myths with origins in ancient times are veritable treasure-houses for any storyteller. The pop culture enthusiasts of the country knew the power of their ancient stories, and they delved deep, found powerful characters and themes, and made contemporary parallels of the mythological elements.

Japanese movies, TV shows, anime, and manga books are all interrelated and interconnected as each item finds inspiration from the others and continue to bring cheer, happiness, and unlimited entertainment to every home in Japan and around the world.

www.DingoPublishing.com

Bonus

As a way of saying thanks for your purchase, we're offering a special gift that's exclusive to my readers.

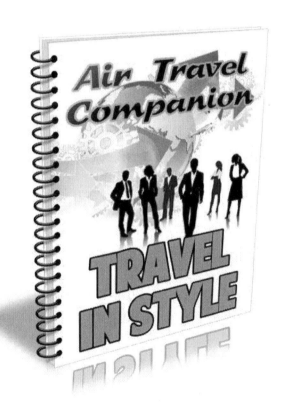

Visit this link below to claim your bonus.

http://dingopublishing.com/bonus/

MORE BOOKS FROM US

Visit our bookstore at: http://www.dingopublishing.com

Below is some of our favorite books:

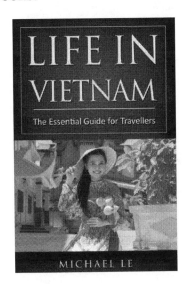

SIMPLE, HEALTHY AND DELICIOUS CHIA SEED RECIPES TO
LIVE LONGER AND FEEL YOUNGER

CHIA SEEDS
Cookbook
Superfoods Every Day

Olivia Green

EASY, HEALTHY AND DELICIOUS KALE RECIPES TO
LIVE LONGER AND FEEL YOUNGER

KALE
Cookbook
Superfoods Every Day

Olivia Green

RAMEN
NOODLES COOKBOOK
The Top 50 Delicious
Ramen Recipes To Cook At Home

LINDA NGUYEN

THE TOP 99 DELICIOUS RECIPES TO
FIGHT CANCER AND RESTORE YOUR HEALTH

ANTI-CANCER
Diet

Olivia Green

DINGO
BOOK CLUB

www.DingoPublishing.com

Thanks again for purchasing this book.

We hope you enjoy it

Don't forget to claim your free bonus:

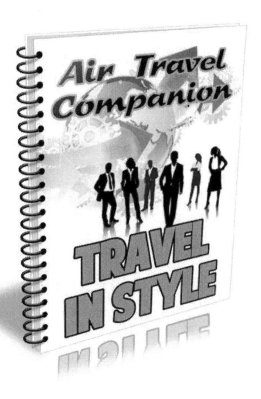

Visit this link below to claim your bonus:

http://dingopublishing.com/bonus/